GREEN TEA

Design: Ann-Sophie Caouette
Illustrations: Marie Bilodeau
Photos: Camellia Sinensis Tea Company
Additional Photography: Olivier Hanigan
Editor: Bruce Richardson
Associate Editors: Sara Loy, Elizabeth Thompson

ISBN 978-0-9836106-6-3

Published in the United States by
Benjamin Press
135 North Second Street
Danville, Kentucky 40422
800.765.2139
BenjaminPress.com

Printed in Canada

GREEN TEA

A QUEST FOR FRESH LEAF AND TIMELESS CRAFT

HUGO AMERICI, JASMIN DESHARNAIS,
FRANÇOIS MARCHAND AND KEVIN GASCOYNE

BENJAMIN PRESS
America's Publisher of Fine Tea Books

TABLE OF CONTENTS

PREFACE

The Western world has once again fallen in love with green tea. For many, drinking green tea has become a new practice spurred by an interest in tea's healthy attributes, while others consider it a ritual that helps balance their busy lives.

Modern tea drinkers are often unaware, however, that Europe and North America once consumed great quantities of green tea, first from China, then Japan, Taiwan, and eventually all of the tea producing countries of Southeast Asia. Bostonians, enraged by taxes levied by George III, tossed seventy-five chests of Chinese Hyson and Singlo teas into the harbor in 1773; Jane Austen drank Chinese green tea during intermission at evening dances in Bath; and in the late 1800s, general stores across America kept their tea bins stocked with fresh Japanese green tea.

Today's green tea advocates are again myriad, but few are as passionate as Hugo Américi, François Marchand, Jasmin Desharnais, and Kevin Gascoyne, a talented quartet of Quebec tea professionals who, for nearly two decades, have developed their much-respected Camellia Sinensis Tea Houses in Montreal and Quebec City. These four gifted teaists are obsessive about their vocation. Each year, they set out to explore the world in search of outstanding teas. Kevin visits India and Sri Lanka, Jasmin and François team up for China, and Hugo heads to Taiwan, Vietnam, and Japan. They return with unique teas and fantastic stories of their adventures in far-off gardens.

As a gift to all of us who love tea, they have assembled various accounts of their experiences in those remote areas where the craft of making tea has been practiced for centuries. Readers will be left with a new understanding of these artisanal teas that, like great wines, exemplify the terroir of their countrysides.

I am pleased to publish this translation from the authors' original French edition entitled *Thé Vert.* Heat the kettle, steep a cup of tea, and prepare to be transported to distant tea gardens in an unending quest for new leaf and timeless craft.

Bruce Richardson, publisher

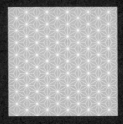

INTRODUCTION

From our earliest exploratory journeys to Asia in search of new terroirs, we have learned much about the complex world of tea. Year after year, treading the paths of those faraway tea gardens, meeting passionate and skillful artisans along the way, we honed our approach to sourcing exceptional teas from skilled artisans.

Our goal has been to integrate the customs and tastes of tea into modern society. Having taken the first steps with our initial book *Tea: History, Terroirs, Varieties*, we now offer a more intimate examination of the fascinating and mysterious world of green tea by highlighting its landscapes, nuances, and spirit.

Through a selection of interviews and first-hand accounts, we share our adventures, our impressions, and tasting notes from many of our recent discoveries.

Welcome to the world of green tea!

Hugo, Jasmin, François, and Kevin

GREEN TEAS AND THE SPRING SEASON

As the first signs of spring announce the rebirth of the tea fields, a sense of excitement stirs amongst the producers. The tea plants are awakening and, reinvigorated by the new season, their fresh shoots burst with aromatic compounds.

In green tea production, the first shoots hold great importance. Their floral and vegetal aromas expand with each inhalation and their deep concentrations of essential oils make their liquors silky while their tannins have just enough presence to sustain harmony and balance.

To benefit from all of these inherent qualities, the leaves must be plucked at the right moment. The producers are on the alert, keeping a close watch on the slightest change in the weather and regularly analyzing the tea plants' growth.

Once the young leaves reach the desired growth-point and the weather conditions are favourable, the harvest becomes a race against the clock. All leaves must be plucked in just a few days. Producers increase their labour force at this time, which draws thousands of migrant pluckers to the tea-growing regions.

The first day of the harvest varies with each year. In China, the earliest harvests usually take place in March before the Qingming ("Day of the Ancestors") festival, which is celebrated around the fifth of April. In the southern provinces, the harvests can begin as early as February.

In Japan, the highly-anticipated first teas of the year are called shincha ("new tea"). Harvested in late April, shincha are celebrated during many festivities and are an integral part of the Japanese rituals that herald the arrival of spring. The Japanese taste for spring freshness is expressed in these lively, vegetal teas.

In both countries, the spring harvest period is spread out over three or four weeks, during which several harvests take place, each a few days apart. Though spring harvests are not necessarily synonymous with quality, in Japan and China, the long-awaited first pick is often the most prestigious.

FIXING THE GREEN

Green tea leaves can be left whole, broken, rolled, flattened, chopped, powdered, or even shaped to look like pine needles. Upon infusion, they reveal colour nuances from pale yellow to spinach green. Some fragrant leaves evoke prairie flowers while others have flavours reminiscent of the sea, seaweed, fresh herbs, or green vegetables. The leaves can be light, gentle, cheerful, and refreshing or acerbic, sharp, brisk, and bitter. Their personalities are countless, but they are all members of the green tea family.

By definition, a green tea consists of non-oxidized leaves. As soon as one plucks a leaf from a tea tree, it naturally begins to wilt: its nature transformed, its pigments slowly turn from green to brown, its compounds beginning to oxidize.

To avoid this natural phenomenon, immediately after the harvest tea producers utilize a procedure where the leaves are heated to neutralize the enzymes that cause the oxidization. This procedure, known as "fixing the green," triggers various chemical reactions that modify the sugars, proteins, and tannin content contained in the leaf.

There are two principal methods used, one typically practiced in China and the other in Japan. As we will see, these two methods produce teas with very different leaf appearances and tastes.

CHINA

The Chinese panning method is ancient. It is carried out using a metal pan heated over a wood fire or, more commonly now, with electricity. The leaves are manually stirred in the pan with a repetitive motion for around twenty minutes before being dried in a second pan.

Various techniques are used to shape the leaves. To obtain a green tea with flat leaves, for example, the leaves are briefly compressed on the bottom of the pan before being stirred with a to-and-fro motion to prevent the leaves from burning. To produce a curly-leafed green tea, the leaves are sporadically rolled between the hands as they are stirred continuously.

Turning the leaves in a pan this way is reserved for high-quality leaves, as only very small quantities can be processed at a time. During more plentiful harvests, manufacturers will use heated, rotating cylinders to mechanically neutralize the enzymes.

The dry heat used in the Chinese method enhances the floral aromas of the tea while retaining the natural vegetal characteristics, often with a roasty hint of hazelnut.

JAPAN

Tea cultivation arrived in Japan from China towards the end of the twelfth century, but few traces of the traditional Chinese transformation techniques remain. Kamairicha is one rare exception; this tea is still produced using the original Chinese panning method. Most Japanese green teas, however, are fixed in a very different way.

In 1738, Soen Nagatani perfected the use of steam to neutralize enzyme activity, which revolutionized the way in which green teas were transformed and which notably led to the creation of Sencha-style teas. In exposing the leaves to jets of hot steam for varying periods of thirty seconds or more, this method has made it possible to produce green teas that distinguish themselves from Chinese green teas in both appearance and flavor profiles.

In addition to conserving the vegetal characteristic often referred to as "fresh grass," the steam treatment creates a tea with the green vegetable aromas and marine notes typical to the Japanese terroir and flavour aesthetic.

CHINA

The great diversity of green teas found throughout China is both phenomenal and bewildering. Centuries of cultivation techniques have yielded a vast spectrum of aromas, from coarse and astringent to sweet and fragrant. Leaf styles differ in a myriad ways as well, with green teas appearing in shapes from tightly-rolled pellets to wide, flattened leaves.

Sold loose in the street or in luxury packaging, and enjoyed by peasants and government officials alike, tea has been a part of Chinese everyday life for generations and remains by far the most consumed beverage in this country.

As we explore new tea-producing regions each year, we find that China is an endless source of discovery. Each region has its specialty and every artisan his or her own special technique. Just as the French wine regions have their legendary grands crus ("great growths"), China's centuries-old tea culture boasts numerous renowned examples that are indicative of the cultivars, terroirs, and production methods of certain regions.

Legendary teas, such as Bi Luo Chun, Long Jing Shi Feng, and Tai Ping Hou Kui, serve as examples of a rich historical lineage. The Chinese are proud of this heritage and the demand for their premium green teas continues to grow steadily. Research centers are being founded to develop new cultivation techniques and mountainsides are being cleared of trees to increase garden areas. Many modern green teas from new cultivars, such as Anji Bai Cha or Jingning Bai Cha, have also burst onto the scene. Production is increasing every year and interest in these new, origin-specific grand cru teas is high. The result is that green tea is more alive than ever in China.

GREEN TEA IN EVERYDAY LIFE

In China's vast train stations, travellers fill their tea flasks and large thermoses for free from one of the many hot water fountains.

The widespread availability of boiling water not only highlights how thoroughly tea consumption is woven into the social fabric, but also reveals an intriguing aspect of Chinese tea culture. In their everyday lives, Chinese consumers are very relaxed about tea preparation as just a few unmeasured leaves are thrown in a glass or tea flask, immersed in boiling water, and re-infused throughout the day.

This easy-going approach has deep roots going all of the way back to the Buddhist and Taoist monks who were the first to cultivate and consume tea for its stimulating properties. The act of drinking tea naturally resonated with the spirit of humility and serenity that embodied their meditation practices. Without necessarily attributing an inherent spiritual value to tea, the monks felt that serving tea was also a way of sharing the values of peace, tranquillity, pleasure, and truth.

This sensibility endures in contemporary Chinese tea drinking. For any Chinese tea enthusiast, consuming tea is naturally associated with the spontaneity and carefree attitude at the core of Taoism. True to this spirit, China has not developed as codified a tea ceremony as one finds, for instance, in Japan.

There is, of course, a more refined side to tea culture in China. In Chinese teahouses, the art of serving tea is very much alive and plays an important role in the social fabric of local communities. In most teashops, one employee, seated at a central table, skillfully infuses tea for clients throughout the day. A great deal of care goes into making each infusion, which is carried out with graceful, studied movements.

Many tea preparation competitions are organized during annual festivals and special events. The participants, almost all of them women, are judged for the grace of their gestures, their attitude, and their beauty, as well as the refinement of their presentation. Two tea-preparation methods are usually presented: the Gong Fu Cha and the gaiwan infusion (see "Preparing Tea in a Gaiwan" pg. 162).

IN SEARCH OF THE ELUSIVE TAI PING HOU KUI

Every tea taster dreams of discovering a remote, virtually inaccessible growing region producing exceptional tea. The discovery of Tai Ping Hou Kui was just such an experience for us.

Since our very first sourcing ventures, this tea had been on our "most wanted" list. Its name was well-known to us, as was the province where it is cultivated, but despite our efforts, we were continually returning empty-handed. Having finally located these lost producers with the help of Mr. Xie, a friend from the tea-producing region of Huang Shan Mao Feng, it became clear why the tea had previously eluded us: there are no roads leading to the gardens of Tai Ping Hou Kui.

Leaving Mr. Xie's home in the magnificent province of Anhui, we had to travel several hours of country roads before stopping on the banks of a river. Because the plantations were not accessible by car, the rest of the journey would have to be made by boat.

The calm waters of the river reflected like a mirror the majestic Huang Shan mountains surrounding it. Having floated through this spectacular landscape for almost an hour, we arrived at the sloping fields of Taiping Hou Kui, one of the most beautiful sites we have had the luck to visit in all our years of sourcing. A patchwork of small tea gardens along the riverside gleamed an enchanting emerald green.

Mr. Ye, the producer we had arranged to meet there, belongs to a long line of producers who have all cultivated tea. The tea trees in his field were all planted by his ancestors. Like the other families in the village, he runs a small factory behind his house. He produces a tea that is characterized by its large, flattened leaves averaging around six centimeters in length. To achieve this remarkable form, Mr. Ye uses an artisanal method of transformation that was completely new to us.

A CRAFTED LEAF

The large-leaf cultivar used for the production of this tea is plucked with great care. With most grand cru teas, only the terminal bud and the two delicate first leaves on the stem are used. For Tai Ping Huo Kui, however, the leaves are allowed to mature a little longer before plucking.

Once plucked, the leaves are sorted and manually fired in a pan for about five minutes.

Rolling is the next step. The leaves are laid out on a fine metal grill one by one with care taken to make sure they do not touch. A second grill is placed

over the leaves. The grills are then set on a wooden table, a cotton cloth laid over the frame, and a hand-held roller passed over the grill with a rapid motion.

The leaves are left in this frame for a final, wood-fired drying. This gradual drying lasts about an hour.

As the leaves' transformation is entirely manual and the terroir's area of cultivation is small, authentic Tai Ping Hou Kui teas are hard to find, even in China. With the rarity and originality of its trademark floral aromas, the Chinese often offer this tea as a gift for special occasions.

LONG JING: THE LEGEND BEHIND ONE OF CHINA'S MOST FAMOUS GREEN TEAS

According to a fourth-century legend, at the far end of the Tianmu Mountains, while drilling a well, inhabitants noticed a rock in the shape of a dragon. This discovery so captured their imaginations that among the mountain folk this well became known as Long Jing, the "Dragon Well."

A few centuries later, the village residents joined forces to build a temple close to the well and the temple attracted many pilgrims from far and wide. A local tea was cultivated for the temple's monks, and it was served to and much appreciated by visitors, who named the tea after the nearby well.

The first Long Jing plantations go back almost fifteen-hundred years to the Tang dynasty [618 – 907]. In 786, in the first book dedicated to tea, Lu Yu's *Classic of Tea* refers to it as "the tea from West Lake." Over the centuries Long Jing's reputation grew until it became the most famous of China's green teas.

Mr. Tang is a member of the current generation of a long line of tea producers established in the village of Long Jing for over three hundred years. Here he talks of how demand has evolved over the course of the twentieth century:

"Before 1949, we only produced our tea to meet the orders of nearby stores. The demand was small. Then, from 1949 to 1979, the village developed a lot. During the Communist period, each family, including mine, received a parcel of land of around five *mu* [0.33 hectare]. Everything that was produced by the residents belonged to the State. In 1979, the State withdrew and let families look after the production and sale of their own teas in the new market economy. But it is only since the beginning of the 1990s that the demand for Long Jing has really skyrocketed. The village producers are no longer able to meet the demand without help. To get maximum yield out of my land, I now need several seasonal workers—six pluckers, most of whom come from outside the village, and Mr. Min, a panning expert—to help me during the high season."

The village of Long Jing's reputation is impressive and its famous tea attracts throngs of tea enthusiasts. During the summer season, thousands of Chinese and foreign tourists visit the region's steep mountains. Throughout this charming village and the surrounding area, there are hiking paths, natural springs, and teahouses where you can drink teas with the families who produce them. For around four dollars, you can buy a generous cupful of fresh leaves that will still be fragrant after several infusions.

With Long Jing's legendary reputation, tea enthusiasts are naturally interested in stocking up on provisions while visiting the site. To meet this ever-increasing demand, the artisans seek to boost production, but as the forests surrounding Long Jing are now part of a national park, they are not able to deforest more of the mountainsides to expand their tea plantations. To protect the park from such activity, the Chinese government is even using satellite surveillance and imposing exemplary fines on producers who fell trees on park land.

Unfortunately, this situation has led to tea counterfeiting. Large harvests from Wunizao, a city in the south of Zhejiang Province, are being sent to Long Jing to be transformed and sold as authentic Long Jing teas. Imitations from other provinces are also frequent. In Sichuan, for example, green tea producers imitate the Long Jing style and take advantage of earlier harvests to capture a large share of the market.

According to Mr. Tang, one of the Long Jing producers' major challenges is to keep prices affordable. It is a problem that is becoming increasingly more difficult to solve. The market price of Long Jing teas, already more expensive than most other teas, continues to increase, and plantation workers' salaries have doubled over the last few years.

To avoid a significant increase in production prices, Mr. Tang (pictured below left with his wife and translator) recently acquired new machines designed to mechanically process an initial firing and reduce the transformation time.

The best Long Jing teas are still transformed manually from start to finish, however. For several years, Mr. Tang has entrusted such delicate work to Mr. Min, who is responsible for the pan-firing stage of his entire production. A man of few words, Mr. Min is one of the many migrant workers who come to the mountainside each year for the production season. Having met him frequently for many years, we had to know more about him and his daily work.

AN INTERVIEW WITH MR. MIN, A LONG JING PANNING EXPERT

Are you originally from Long Jing?
No, I am from the city of Luan in Anhui Province.

Why do you come to Long Jing every year?
I receive a better salary in Long Jing. For the same number of work hours, I make about four times as much as I do back in Anhui, plus room and board are provided. Even more, I love the mountain surroundings here. It's so quiet and very charming in the spring.

What is your work schedule like?
During the harvest season, I work every day, unless it rains.

What do you do the rest of the year?
I am a construction worker.

How did you learn the panning technique?
Mr. Tang's father taught me the finer points of manual panning. I learned the traditional method.

What do you like about this work?
The smell of the leaves. I also like the feel of the leaves in the hot pan.

Aside from Long Jing, what is your favourite tea?
My favourite tea comes from Anhui; it is Huo Shan Huang Ya.

HUANG SHAN MAO FENG
AND THE CULTURAL REVOLUTION

Anhui Province is home to the magnificent Huang Shan ("Yellow Mountains"). With their granite peaks, ancient pine trees, brilliant sunsets, and famous "sea of clouds," this area is one of China's most inspiring topographical regions. For centuries monks, artists, and aesthetes from all over China have frequented Huang Shan in search of illumination, inspiration, or solitude.

Tea was first harvested in Huang Shan in the middle of the Ming dynasty [1368-1644]. During this era, the tea was called Huang Shan Yun Wu, the "Night and Mist of Yellow Mountain." The creation of Huang Shan Mao Feng, the "New Shoots of Yellow Mountain," goes back to the end of the nineteenth century. This tea's delicate leaves, subtle vegetal notes, and supple liquor have earned it a place amongst China's classic green teas.

Mr. Xie and his family made their home on a small plateau on the mountain. As producers of Huan Shan Mao Feng, they endured many difficult years before enjoying great success. For a clearer understanding of their situation, we must first reopen a difficult chapter in China's history: the Cultural Revolution.

Launched by China's first Communist leader Chairman Mao Zedong in 1966, the Cultural Revolution was a period of major upheavals for China. One of its revolutionary goals was to eradicate the traditional cultural values of the Chinese people. Anything described as celebrated or precious was henceforth considered bourgeois and materialist, and therefore against the Mao regime's philosophy. As a long-established aspect of Chinese society, tea culture was not to be spared.

With the Communists in power, private companies were transformed into State corporations. For the tea producers, the consequences were immediate: selling tea to private entities became illegal. No longer able to live off his tea crop, Mr. Xie's father was forced to go to work as a teacher in another

province. Though tea continued to be cultivated in Huang Shan, all production was standardized and distributed throughout the country.

The Cultural Revolution officially ended in 1976, but it was not until the beginning of the 1980s that economic reform put an end to the State-controlled system of tea production. The tea gardens were once again parceled out and the peasant families reclaimed their land.

In 1988, to revive the heritage of his ancestors, Mr. Xie rebuilt the tea factory at Huang Shan. He reclaimed his father's gardens and set about revitalizing the production of Huang Shan Mao Feng.

When we first met him in 2004, Mr. Xie worked in a small factory behind his house where he transformed his tea manually using traditional methods. Since then, the business has undergone astonishing growth. A strong demand for Huang Shan Mao Feng enabled Mr. Xie to increase his production and to build the modern factory he now operates with his son. He even has to buy fresh leaves for the factory from neighbouring gardens just to meet the demand.

He is very proud to have saved his family's tea producing tradition.

THE JADE SPIRALS OF SPRING

The grands crus are naturally the first teas to be presented in most books on tea. Having charmed the local populations over centuries, they now entice foreign enthusiasts and enjoy international renown.

Approaching the world of green teas by tasting a grand cru is not a bad idea, but neophytes can often benefit from a little guidance to best appreciate its subtleties.

Bi Luo Chun is a perfect example. A full appreciation of this green tea from Jiangsu Province can be particularly challenging. Its tiny leaves and down-covered buds are renowned for their strong "dizzying perfume."[1] The infusion must be carried out with great care as the aromatic power of these small curly leaves quickly develops a dense astringency that can overwhelm the vegetal freshness and the fruity subtlety of its liquor, leaving the drinker disheartened. When its rich and complex character is unleashed through optimal infusion conditions, however, the qualities that make it a grand cru tea are unmistakable. Bi Luo Chun remains China's most celebrated tea after Long Jing.

Produced in very limited quantities during the first spring harvests around the end of March, Bi Luo Chun is one of the rare Chinese teas that is still manufactured entirely by hand as it has been for centuries.

Mr. Liu, our Bi Luo Chun producer, cultivates tea trees in the sandy earth of the terraced slopes of his garden. The old stone walls supporting the

---

1. Bi Luo Chun's legendary perfume derives from its exceptionally small leaves and large quantity of buds. This tea's former name was Xia Sha Ren Xiang, meaning "the tea with the dizzying smell." Emperor Kang Xi [1661 – 1722] preferred the more elegant name of Bi Luo Chun or "Jade Spiral" however, and it has carried that name now for over three hundred years.

terraces bristle with weeds. Apricot trees also grow in the garden, and osmanthus bushes are planted in strategic spots to lure insects away from the tea plants.

The Bi Luo Chun leaves are some of the smallest green tea shoots we have ever seen. This makes their harvest quite demanding. An experienced picker can only harvest a very small 300 to 500 grams of green leaves per day. After picking, the leaves are withered on bamboo racks and the firing is done in pans heated by wood fires.

Since the leaves are transformed manually, the artisans' craft is fundamental to the process. The subtleties of manufacture are measured by human interaction; for instance, to test whether the leaves have lost enough humidity for panning, a fistful of leaves is squeezed in the hand. If the leaves cling like dough, they are not yet ready.

Heating a pan with a wood fire also requires a lot of experience. The temperature must be rigorously controlled for the twenty to thirty minutes it takes to stir the leaves with a repetitive motion. If the pan gets too hot, the leaves will scorch. One person will stoke and tend the fire continually while another completes the panning process.

The highest grades of Bi Luo Chun have become a rarity in China. To satisfy the thirst for such teas, Mr. Liu also produces more affordable options, such as Dong Shan, made with handpicked leaves and mechanically transformed.

DONG SHAN AND BI LUO CHUN: A COMPARISON

Dong Shan tea is produced using leaves from the same trees in the same gardens as Bi Luo Chun. Despite sharing the same terroir, these two teas are very different. Comparing their properties precisely illustrates the difference between a grand cru and an everyday tea.

First, the Dong Shan leaves are uniform and dark green. They have none of the fine white down we see from the Bi Luo Chun buds. This is the principal difference: the quality of the plant material used.

Second, Bi Luo Chun is made with a very careful selection of the first and earliest spring shoots when the buds are downy, while Dong Shan is

picked later in the season when the leaves are maturing and no longer have the same aromatic sparkle.

The mechanically-transformed Dong Shan leaves are also put through a faster and hotter panning process than Bi Luo Chun leaves, which changes their flavour. To the well-trained nose, Dong Shan reveals less delicate aromas and the slightly roasted edge typical in mechanically-transformed tea.

Both Bi Luo Chun and Dong Shan can be seen as quality products, however. The trusty everyday tea and the finest grand cru should both be appreciated for their different inherent properties.

THE BAI YE CULTIVAR
AND THE BEAUTY OF THE LEAVES

Despite the power of tradition, the world of green tea is evolving rapidly in China. The last few years have been particularly eventful. On the botanical front, many new cultivars have been created and tested for an increased yield or to produce teas adapted to modern tastes.

Bai Ye No. 1 is amongst the newest fashionable cultivars. It has been cultivated only since the 1990s, but its renown has spread well beyond Anji County in Zhejiang Province, where it originates. It was named "white leaf" after the pale yellow, almost white colour of its leaves, which are distinctly marked by a green central vein.

Early in the harvest season, plantation sections planted with Bai Ye No. 1 are easily distinguished from those planted with other tea plants by their golden shimmer in the sunlight. Later in the season, as they mature, the leaves will develop the deep forest green hues typical of other cultivars.

Aside from the surprising colour of this cultivar, the leaves produce infusions that are markedly less tannic, as in the case of the Bai Ye No. 1 tea, Anji Bai Cha. With its attractive pine needle-shaped leaves and its delicate flavour, Anji Bai Cha became popular rapidly, so much so that producers from northern Zhejiang currently cannot meet the demand. Each year, producers from other provinces take advantage of this situation by clearing forests to increase the size of their gardens and planting Bai Ye No. 1 to produce their own Anji Bai Cha.

Anji Bai Cha's attractive appearance is one of the principal reasons that it has become one of China's most prominent teas in only a few years. The Chinese are fascinated by tea's visual aesthetic. In addition to appreciating the form and the colour of the leaves, they also have a strong appreciation for the leaves' movements in the water during infusion. The most sought-after leaves are those that rest parallel to the sides of a glass.

Bai Ye No. 1 meets all of these aesthetic requirements so perfectly that producers do not want to cultivate Bai Ye No. 2, which was recently developed by tea researchers. The leaves of this new cultivar do not unfurl as beautifully in the water as those of Bai Ye No. 1.

THE POETRY OF LUSHAN YUN WU

Benevolent breezes intimately embrace pearly tea shoots,
The early spring coaxing out buds of golden yellow.
Picked fresh, fired 'til fragrant, then packed and sealed:
Tea's essence and goodness is preserved.
Such venerable tea is meant for princes and nobles;
How did it reach the hut of this mountain hermit?

An excerpt from the poem "Writing Thanks to Imperial Grand Master of Remonstrance Meng for Sending New Tea" by Lu Tung

This is how the ninth-century poet Lu Tung expressed himself in one of the most famous Chinese poems about tea. Lu Tung, well-known as a tea fanatic, spent most of his time drinking tea and reciting poetry about his passion, phrased so beautifully here as "buds of golden yellow." Whether celebrating the beauty of springtime, the purity of a spring's water, or the efforts of a difficult harvest, in China the world of tea has always been imbued with and enhanced by poetry.

Tea in general is a reoccurring theme in Chinese literature, and some teas, such as Lushan Yun Wu, have been a particularly strong source of inspiration for writers and poets. Cultivated on Lushan Mountain, famous for its breathtaking landscapes and for the ancient Xilin Temple, Lushan Yun Wu was first praised by poet Bai Juyi [772-846] in his poem "A Visit to Xilin Temple in Spring."

A VISIT TO XILIN TEMPLE IN SPRING

I dismount from my horse at Xilin Temple;
I throw the porter my slender riding-whip.
In the morning I work at a government office desk;
In the evening I become a dweller in the Sacred Hills.
In the second month, to the north of Lushan Mountain,
The ice breaks and the snow begins to melt.
On the southern plantation the tea plants thrust up their shoots;
Through the northern sluice, the veins of the spring ooze.

Bai Juyi

As with any mountainous environment, on Lushan Mountain weather conditions are not always favourable for tea plants. In the past, when tea was produced as part of the tribute paid to the emperor, bad weather could have terrible consequences. Even today the climate can be a formidable enemy. In the following poem, poet Liao Yu evokes the peasants' helplessness against the unpredictability of nature.

A TEA BALLAD

Usually the tea harvest takes place earlier.
This year it was delayed.
April, and a cold wind still blows on the boulders, the clouds are freezing.
For ten days now we have been going about with our baskets empty.
One day it is beautiful, and we hurry to pick the tea leaves.
There are few leaves to pick; wild pigs have eaten half of them.
We sigh and return to the temple.
We are told that a visitor has arrived in town.
A mandarin bearing a bill for a hundred and sixty dan of Lushan tea.
On the bill it is written that the tea must be picked before Gu Yu,
That the tea must have a pleasing colour and the subtle fragrance of an orchid.
A three-day delay.
The old, grey-haired monk tells his disciples:
"The tea leaves are few, but I entrust to you
*   the task of hiring hands for the harvest."*

Liao Yu

Tea is known as "the drink of the immortals" and Chinese literature abounds with passages celebrating its ability to increase longevity. Is it due to its taste, the mysteries of its production, or the efforts of the peasants who cultivate it that tea holds such properties? In the following poem, poet Sanli Chen [1853-1937] imagines tea as a panacea, "a cure for all ills."

LUSHAN YUN WU TEA

Do you see the tea plants on Lushan Mountain?
Because over there it is cold; the buds appear only in May.

Neither the sun nor the moon can reach some of its land;
The wind and the earth nourish the tea plants.

The monks could injure their legs while picking the leaves,
On top of risking an attack by a tiger or leopard.

The monks offered a tea that purified me;
A spoon, a bowl, and I feel immortal.

I would like to bring some back, to infuse it
With the water from the Four Oceans' springs.

With this infusion, I will be protected from injuries
And against the winter cold and summer heat.

Sanli Chen

This short selection of poems holds testimony to the deep, rich fascination that Lushan Yun Wu tea instills in the Chinese. Its taste, virtues, and mysteries have inspired a great school of poetry deeply rooted in the natural and cultural landscape. Thanks to this tea, these poets continue to travel in the here and now, inspiring modern tea lovers today.

THE EXTRAORDINARY LU AN GUA PIAN

The Chinese are a generous and welcoming people. We were again reminded of this by Mr. Cheng, a grower of Huo Shan Huang Ya in Anhui Province. Eager to help us in our tea sourcing, he insisted on taking us to a village nearby to meet a grower of Lu An Gua Pian.

The road to the Lu An Gua Pian gardens winds its way through the Dabie Shan mountains; it is lined with bamboo forests, small villages, and magnificent lakes. We were captivated by these landscapes, curious to meet the artisans, and excited to discover the original terroir of one of China's ten most famous teas.

We arrived with summer in full swing. The tea trees shimmered in the glorious sunshine. Following a warm welcome, Mr. Deng, a producer of Lu An Gua Pian, invited us on a walk through the gardens, where groups of female pluckers were busy at work.

During our many years of travelling for tea, we have often been impressed by the originality exemplifid in many regions' cultivation and manufactuing techniques. However, the unique techniques employed for the production of Lu An Gua Pian are amongst the most interesting we have ever seen.

Usually, for the production of high-quality teas, one only picks the terminal bud and the first leaf or two. In the case of Lu An Gua Pian, it is not the youngest shoots that are picked, but rather the five to eight leaves that follow the first leaf of each stem.

Once plucked, the leaves are withered on bamboo racks. They then undergo a two-step panning procedure. The leaves are first turned for fifteen minutes in a hot pan. They are then transferred to another, cooler pan, where they are flattened with a small broom.

The subsequent drying stage is also quite original. The artisans pan the leaves over a wood fire, then turn them every fifteen to twenty seconds. This action, Mr. Deng explains, must be carried out for about an hour.

In addition to being quite demanding, this turning action causes many of the precious tea leaves to fall to the ground. We were intrigued, as was Mr. Cheng, who asked Mr. Deng, "Why are you doing this? You are losing far too much tea. Look at all these wasted leaves on the ground!"

With a big smile, Mr. Deng replied that Lu An Gua Pian has been made like this for generations and this is how it must be made.

This amusing exchange nicely illustrates the extent to which transformation methods can differ within the same province and demonstrates just how important the artisans' skills are in the creation of each tea's distinguishing features. The final result is an original tea, Lu An Gua Pian, which has been amongst China's most renowned teas for centuries.

TEAHOUSES IN CHINA:
IMPORTANT GATHERING PLACES

From the Song dynasty [960-1279] until the first half of the twentieth century, teahouses were widespread throughout China. Having all but disappeared, teahouses have been returning in great numbers since the 1990s.

In his well-known play *The Teahouse*, playwright Lao She [1899-1966] writes:

"In the teahouses, one heard the most absurd stories, such as how in a certain place a huge spider had turned into a demon and was then struck by lightning. One could also come in contact with the strangest opinions—for example, the opinion that foreign troops could be prevented from landing by building a great wall along the coast. Here one might also hear about the latest tune composed by some Beijing Opera star or the best way to prepare opium. In the teahouses, one might also see rare art objects newly acquired by some patron: a jade fan pendant recently unearthed or a three-coloured glazed snuffbox. Yes, the teahouse was indeed an important place; it could even be reckoned a kind of cultural centre."

Teahouses played an important role in the everyday lives of many citizens. They were gathering places conducive to exchange, like cafés in continental Europe and pubs in England. With the advent of Mao's Cultural Revolution, almost all of the teahouses had to close. Drinking tea at one of these establishments was considered an idle activity and therefore contrary to the regime's interests. It was also feared that spending time drinking at teahouses could encourage counter-revolutionary ideas to emerge.

Teahouses are now reappearing with renewed vigour, however. Once again they play the role they had enjoyed before the arrival of the Communist regime and are becoming an integral part of the face of modern China, with its booming economy and increasing wealth. Teahouses we have had the opportunity of visiting during our travels display a certain stylistic unity that varies only subtly from region to region.

THE TEAHOUSES OF THE COASTAL PROVINCES

The big cities along the coast were the first to launch the trend of constructing luxurious teahouses. Reputable architects and designers continue to push their creativity to the limit as they compete to build increasingly extravagant establishments. Solid wood tables, wooden bridges, exotic lanterns, displays of calligraphy, and a wide range of sculptures and exhibitions demonstrate the works of well-known artists. The decorations in the teahouses of the coastal provinces are both luxurious and elegant. The biggest establishments have private suites for important functions. They also offer expansive buffets. Young women serve the tea with studied grace, adding to the harmony of the warm and relaxing ambiance.

People gather in these places for business, pleasure, or to search for inspiration. Some engage in heated debates, while others savour a famous tea or sample regional specialties. One can easily stay all day, enjoying the ambiance and tucking into the buffet, as long as one drinks at least one tea per session. A day at a teahouse is generally divided into two sessions: the first beginning around noon when the doors open and lasting until 6 pm, the second from 6 pm until closing time after midnight. One tea generally costs between twelve and twenty dollars, but prices for rare teas can be upwards of a thousand.

THE TEAHOUSES OF SICHUAN

Of all the provinces, Sichuan is probably the one with the most teahouses. Its capital, Chengdu, has over a hundred. Throughout the province these establishments can be found everywhere, both in the city and the countryside, in public spaces, along waterways, and in parks. These teahouses are amongst the most entertaining in the country and are enjoyed by tea drinkers of all ages and social classes.

The desire to maintain Chinese culture is more pronounced in Sichuan teahouses than in anywhere else. Traditional shows, with music, shadow the-

atre, mask changing dances, and other such events, are regularly presented; storytellers and poets perform in these spaces as well. Occasionally, original performances linked to tea culture, or big shows with dancers and countless extras, can be viewed. The teahouse employees manipulate their unusual copper teapots with extended spouts almost a meter in length, assuming theatrical, acrobatic positions as they pour boiling water into each gaiwan.

Some of the teahouses we visited in Sichuan can seat several hundred people, while others, far more simple and modest, offer typical regional specialties on their humble street-side terraces.

THE DEMOCRATIZATION
OF WHITE TEAS

Similar to green tea, these teas are non-oxidized with a subtle and delicate flavour. Often characterized by their downy buds and large whole leaves, they yield an aromatic spectrum particularly appealing to enthusiasts of mild and understated teas. Though only a few varieties exist, they are all part of a very distinct family: the white teas.

There is nothing quite like a cold beverage on a hot summer's day, and yet many teas can be just as refreshing. This is notably the case for white teas. In cities with scorching summers, such as Hong Kong and Beijing, the white tea Bai Mu Dan is popular for its thirst-quenching properties.

Bai Mu Dan was the original white tea, first appearing during the Song dynasty. Emperor and tea enthusiast Huizong, who ruled China between 1100 and 1125, mentions it in his *Treatise on Tea*. According to one legend, only young glove-clad girls were chosen to pick these leaves, their imagery evoking the purity and freshness that emanates from the tea's delicate buds. As with all of the kingdom's greatest fineries, this white tea was reserved for the emperor alone.

The Bai Hao Yin Zhen tea that we know today is produced in a more modern way. It is comprised entirely of buds whose trademark shape and colour are easily recognizable. Due to its beautiful appearance, it was called Yin Zhen, "Silver Needles," towards the end of the eighteenth century. Since then its floral aspects and mild, silky liquor have won the hearts of tea enthusiasts worldwide.

The visual beauty of this white tea is attributed to an indigenous cultivar, the Fuding Da Bai or "Big White," discovered in its wild state in 1857 in the mountains near the city of Fuding in Fujian Province. Its growth period from early March to mid-November is longer than the average cultivar and its robust, downy silver buds have the advantage of remaining tender for a longer time than most. Though also used in black and green tea production, Fuding Da Bai has an ideal bud for white tea.

Depending on the spring weather conditions, the Bai Hao Yin Zhen harvest is spread out over a ten to fifteen day period. Only undamaged and unopened buds are selected. Around forty-thousand buds, all handpicked, are required for the production of a single kilo of Bai Hao Yin Zhen.

In China, the three counties traditionally known for the quality of their white teas are Fuding, Zhenghe, and Jianyang, all located in Fujian Province. Other provinces, notably Hunan, have taken advantage of the strong demand, however, and have begun developing their own white teas. The enthusiasm for white tea has also spread beyond China. Many other countries, such as India, Sri Lanka, Nepal, and even Malawi, are now producing their own variations.

The white tea category of Bai Mu Dan remains popular today and is increasingly present on the market. Unlike Bai Hao Yin Zhen, which contains only buds, these teas are made up of buds and leaves. Certain inferior grades even consist of nothing but broken leaves. With their slightly woody, straw-like aromas and more affordable prices, Bai Mu Dan teas have helped to contribute to the democratization of the once-exclusive white teas.

THE EMPEROR'S COLOUR

In traditional Chinese culture, yellow is the imperial colour. Often used in the clothing of emperors, this colour is considered to have a noble and sacred quality. According to legend, yellow teas were given the lofty name they bear in order to honour the emperor. While the rarity of yellow teas once endowed them with a certain nobility, the "yellow" designation is now reserved for teas that have been fermented through a "smothering" technique. This transformation process results in leaves that have a subtle yellow hue.

Smothering, also known as post-fermentation, is carried out after an initial firing and consists of covering the leaves with a bamboo paper or cotton cloth. The moist heat given off by smothering the leaves triggers a bacterial reaction that gives the leaves their singular colour. Depending on the ambient temperature, the smothering stage can last between eight and twenty hours. Two or three more of these fermentations are applied, separated by intervals of several hours of cooling and reheating. A final drying of ten to twenty minutes completes the transformation.

Despite the love the people of China have for rare and prestigious things, the production of yellow tea is a tradition that has lost much of its popularity. Modern consumers are less enamored by its colour and slightly acidic character. Compared to the enthusiasm roused by some of the most exceptional green teas, yellow teas lack the attention they deserve. Amongst the three "official" examples of yellow tea, Huo Shan Huang Ya from Anhui Province has practically disappeared. Due to a lack of demand, many growers have had to adapt their production to suit the current market. The typical yellow tea transformation methods have now been modified so that the leaves retain their green tones. As a consequence, most of the Huo Shan Huang Ya teas on the market are now actually green teas.

This same phenomenon also applies to Meng Ding Huang Ya, a yellow tea from Sichuan. Despite its reputation, the colour of its buds—less vivid than that of green teas—has led to a decreasing market interest. To respond to this change, the producers have developed from it Meng Ding Gan Lu, a green tea that is more vibrant when infused in a glass.

Nevertheless, Meng Ding Huang Ya has a very distinct taste and growers have every reason to be proud of this yellow tea. It takes three successive fermentations to produce it, each lasting about ten to twelve hours. Between the first and second fermentations, the leaves are heated and rolled using a straw broom to remove the down from the buds. Once finished, Meng Ding Huang Ya has a delicate sweetness with predominant notes of hazelnut.

Despite its faded popularity, yellow tea continues to be highly respected in China and abroad. Jun Shan Yin Zhen—found only in a single, charming terroir in the middle of Lake Dongting in Hunan Province—is one such respected tea. Once reserved only for the emperor during the Song dynasty [960-1279], this tea grows on the small island of Jun Shan ("the Emperor's Mountain"), which is completely covered in tea plants.

The annual production of the highest grade of this legendary tea is limited to sixty kilos, making it one of the world's rarest teas. Great attention is thus paid to the picking of the buds that go into its production. Only the buds that have not been damaged by wind, rain, or insects are selected. The artisanal producers even remove any bud that has not grown perfectly straight.

The imperial harvests of Jun Shan Yin Zhen take place in the springtime before the Qingming festival in early April. Whatever is picked after this celebration is used to produce Jun Shan Huang Mao Jian, a less celebrated tea that consists of buds and leaves. Even though the principal teas from Jun Shan are their yellow teas, green teas are also produced there to meet demand.

Today Jun Shan Yin Zhen is considered amongst the ten most famous teas of China. It continues to fascinate Chinese enthusiasts with its delicate, straight, and downy buds and the suggestion it conjures up of a bamboo forest when infused.

ZHU YE QING,
THE SACRED TEA OF SICHUAN

Zhu Ye Qing first appeared in tea history in the early 1960s. Its creation is attributed to a monk who lived on top of Mount Emei. In 1964, the government minister Chen Yi gave the tea its name, meaning "Green Bamboo Leaf," during his visit to the mountain's oldest temple, the Temple of Ten Thousand Years.

Mount Emei, where Zhu Ye Qing is grown, is one of Buddhism's four sacred mountains in China. The first Buddhist temple to be built in the country is located there, as well as many monasteries that draw thousands of pilgrims each year in search of religious revelations and mystical experiences. The Sea of Clouds, which shrouds the landscape between the rocky peaks, and the famous Buddha's Light, an amazing light-refraction phenomenon, have made this area a popular tourist destination.

Tea gardens have been cultivated on Mount Emei's slopes since ancient times. We have always noticed that the people of Sichuan, in both the cities and the countryside, consume a peculiarly copious amount of tea, far in excess of the citizens of other Chinese provinces. In the streets and in the many teahouses, green tea is still served in large gaiwan rather than in glasses, which has become customary elsewhere in China.

Due to Sichuan's wet, sub-tropical climate, teas can be plucked and produced relatively early in the year. The first harvests usually begin in mid-February, which is why the first spring teas available on the market often come from this province.

Zhu Ye Qing is the best-known Sichuan green tea. Its dark green leaves are flattened and stylishly formed. Connoisseurs will often infuse this tea in a glass just for the pleasure of observing their smooth lines and down-free clarity. Zhu Ye Qing is indeed one of the Chinese green teas that is the most beautiful to observe.

Many pilgrims visit Mount Emei to contemplate Buddha's Light while savouring the brisk flavour of Zhu Ye Qing. The remarkable spectacle unfolding before their eyes naturally leads them to endow the tea itself with mysterious and sacred qualities.

AN INTERVIEW WITH MS. ZHOU, A TEA PRODUCER

We met this producer (pictured right) during our first exploration of Sichuan while searching for Zhu Ye Qing. Surprised to see a woman in her thirties heading a family tea company, we find out more about her vision of Chinese tea production.

How long has your family been working in the world of tea?

My grandfather was a businessman who produced and sold tea. My father grew tea solely for personal consumption. When I began in 1996, everything was done by hand. I hoped to make a living from it. Today, we have a semi-artisanal factory and the entire family participates in the company. My parents live in the countryside and manage everything related to the harvest and transformation of the tea. My brother, sister, and I take care of the sales.

Is it difficult to be a woman in the world of tea?

There are still far more men than women in the world of tea, but this is not always a disadvantage for me. Physically, it is very demanding work, especially when the days are long and you still have to take care of all sorts of commercial issues. It is in moments like this, however, that a woman is often more meticulous and patient.

Do you prefer experimenting with tea or continuing the tradition?

I like experimenting with new teas. In addition to my main tea, Zhu Ye Qing, I am developing other teas similar to Bi Luo Chun, Long Jing, Huang Ya, and Bai Hao Yin Zhen.

In your opinion, what will the world of tea be like in China in ten years?

I think that more and more young people of my generation like to drink tea. Many tea-flavoured products, such as mooncakes, candies, and sunflower seeds, are also very popular with youth. As I see it, tea is currently in a major expansion period in China. The Chinese are just beginning to take advantage of a more comfortable lifestyle. Since 2004, the tea market has experienced amazing growth. In ten years, I believe it will be even bigger.

FIRST ENCOUNTER

Guizhou is one of China's least developed provinces. Its breathtaking mountains and lime-stone features give it an undeniable charm. The region does not have a single "famous tea," but rather several lesser-known productions grown in the isolated high mountains.

When one explores new regions, the search for the right producers is always a challenge. Foreign language barrier aside, with each new encounter we must introduce ourselves and explain our approach as tea importers specializing in direct import from the source. We then have to help them understand the reality of our market, which is quite different from the Chinese market.

That being said, building a good business relationship with a producer is not simply based on our discovering an excellent tea. As well as the human connection, we are also looking for authentic manufacture based on quality and a respect for the environment. These are all essential elements in our list of selection criteria.

When we visit a production region for the first time, we usually make an effort to meet several producers in order to find one with whom we would like to develop a long-term relationship. In Guizhou, luck was on our side when we met Mr. Li and Ms. Chen, welcoming, curious, and passionate people who very much share our tea philosophy.

We first got to know Ms. Chen in Guiyang, the capital of Guizhou, where she introduced herself while preparing three green teas infusions in gaiwan. Without being aware of it, Ms. Chen had already impressed us with her professionalism. Though the gaiwan is an essential tool for tasters, as it assists in revealing the hidden subtleties of certain teas, it is rarely used for daily green tea preparation anymore. Most modern producers and consumers will infuse their green teas in glasses to best appreciate its appearance.

Mr. Li and his wife Ms. Chen work together in the company they founded back in 2000. She takes care of the business and their tea store while he focuses on the production. This small family operation produces several dozen grades of Du Yun Mao Jian, a tightly-curled tea similar in form to the famous Bi Luo Chun. The entirely manual transformation of the first flush spring grades endows them with a very delicate vegetal quality and velvety texture. The secondary grades undergo a mechanical firing. The large majority of their production is destined for the local market.

Having finished our first tasting session, we took the road to Duyun to visit their plantation. Duyun is a two-hour drive from the capital, with another two hours through dazzling mountainous landscapes to reach the gardens.

Arriving at the foot of their plantation, we spotted the small factory where Mr. Li transforms his harvests. Naturally we were keen to look around, but he demonstrated a noticeable amount of hesitation before agreeing to take us there. With brand image so crucial in China, his hesitation was understandable. Big, flashy new factories are the ones that promote sales here, as Chinese buyers attach a great deal of importance to modern installations and the impression of success they display. Mr. Li excused himself several times for the simplicity of his equipment, though we were fascinated and impressed by their authenticity and artisanal aspect. We knew full well, after all, that expensive installations are not necessarily synonymous with quality.

Following this and a series of visits to other growers in the region, we made our way back to Guiyang to continue our tasting sessions and to complete our purchases.

In Ms. Chen's store, we prepared to taste around fifteen Du Yun Mao Jian teas of various grades. Unlike many other producers, who enjoy this moment by wandering off to smoke a cigarette or two, Ms. Chen honoured us by participating in the tasting session and sharing her sensory impressions of each infusion. Presented with this impressive selection, we discussed the characteristics of each tea before making our choice: a superior grade with numerous buds from a first-rate pluck and a regular grade with a more brisk flavour, perfect for an everyday tea. Given that Du Yun Mao Jin is not a well-known tea, the asking price for this kind of quality is extremely reasonable.

As is customary in China, in the evening we ate dinner together at a restaurant before finishing off our business. Accompanied by Chinese buyers from Sichuan also interested in doing business with Ms. Chen, we enjoyed a lively and colorful theatrical show put on by members of the Buyi ethnic minority.

CELADON GREEN

Located in the southwest of Zhejiang Province, the city of Longquan is one of the most important centres of Chinese ceramics. It is also the cradle of celadon. This locally-developed glazing technique makes it possible to create objects in tones of jade, the sacred stone so highly prized in Asia. Popular today for their light and pleasing hues, celadon bowls are ideal for tea drinking.

According to recent archeological research, which has uncovered more than five hundred ancient kilns, the ceramic history of Longquan goes back to the fifth century. The first pieces made were bowls with a very thick, yellow-green half-glaze.

During the Song dynasty, the golden age of celadon, the perfection of the manufacturing process and increased control over firing temperatures made it possible to produce objects such as jars, pots, plates, and vases with purer forms and a semi-transparent, shiny, crack-free glaze.

With its nuanced shades wonderfully echoed by those of green tea, celadon won the favour of many Chinese scribes. Not only did this esteem spread to the imperial court, but it also fostered the development of this style of pottery in several other countries, including Korea, where potters have also attained a high level of celadon mastery.

As for Chinese celadon, there are two main types: the white-green type, with its glossy and semi-transparent effect obtained by applying several layers of glaze, and the crackled type, which is produced through the modification of the glaze formula so as to vary its expansion coefficient. The glaze's characteristic green is determined by its iron oxide content, which reacts during down-firing. Potters are also able to vary the green hues by controlling the cooling temperature.

Modern celadon objects come in a wide range of textures and colours, from bowls as delicate as the finest porcelain to chunky cups with thick glazes.

AN INTERVIEW WITH MR. YEN WEI EN,
A POTTER FROM LONGQUAN

In his workshop, which is surrounded by a magnificent garden decorated with art-
work, we met Mr. Yen, a potter and calligrapher. During this encounter, we found
out a great deal about this artist and his mindset and were able to discover the
place that brings him inspiration and tranquility.

Mr. Yen, how did you become a potter?

*I came from a family of potters and was therefore born into this milieu. From 1988 to 1992,
I was a student in the fine arts department of the Celadon Institute in Jingdezheng. I have
worked as a potter ever since.*

In your opinion, what are the qualities of a good potter?

*A good potter must have good technical skills. He must also know philosophy, aesthetics,
history, culture, and traditional ceramics. The Chinese greatly respect artisans that possess
knowledge and virtue, for benevolence is the soul of art. In my view, morality and know-how
are important qualities for a potter.*

Do you do research and experimentation?

*I am always researching and experimenting because I am curious and I like to learn new
techniques. My ambition is to create pottery that suits today's tastes while still including elements of traditional culture. I hope one day to have my own store and my own line of pottery
so that my works may be appreciated throughout the world.*

Do you think there are elements or conditions that escape the potter?

*No matter how skilled or experienced a potter is, several elements influence the completion
of a work: the materials, temperature, and water quality. These uncontrollable factors are
part of the pleasure of creating.*

What is your view of the art of ceramics in contemporary China?

*In China, the skill level amongst potters is uneven. There aren't many impressive works. Far
too many potters are more concerned with short-term profit. For several years, I wavered on
this point. I now create my works with the heart of an artisan.*

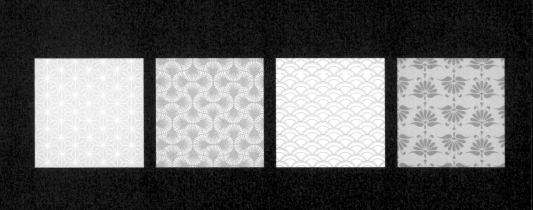

JAPAN

In Japan, tea was a ritual beverage long before it became part of an aesthetic, a philosophy, or a way to give
expression to the principal aspects of Japanese society. Amongst all of the tea-producing countries of the
world, Japan has managed to distinguish itself through
its highly-original, formalized tea culture.

Green tea holds a prominent place in contemporary
Japan. Almost all tea production there is dedicated to
green tea, and many tea traditions live on in Japan today. Shade growing is still practiced, traditions of manual leaf transformation continue, and the Japanese tea
ceremony remains an expression of a way of life that
influences a variety of artistic disciplines, including pottery, architecture, and flower arrangement.

More than any other country, sophisticated modern
cultivation and transformation techniques have been
perfected in Japan, revealing the full potential of this
remarkable terroir. With an increasing diversification of
products linked to green tea, Japan is also a place where
new cultivars are constantly being developed, the earth
is fertilized in innovative ways, and remarkable ingenuity goes into the production of their grand cru teas.

STEAM AND FIRE

For a Japanese green tea enthusiast, the world of Sencha is fascinating. More than seventy percent of all Japanese tea production is reserved for Sencha. This tea comes in all levels of quality and presents a wide range of sub-styles and aromatic profiles. Understanding the subtle variations in transformation techniques used for Sencha and the tasting parameters they create can help us to better select and enjoy the possibilities of this style.

The two essential elements for Sencha transformation are steam (for the fixing) and fire (for the roasting). The flavour and aromatic value of this tea is to a large extent a result of these two processes.

As previously mentioned, fixing the natural enzymes in the leaves with heat is essential to keeping a green tea green. Without it, the leaves would oxidize and quickly become useless. In Japan, this fixing is usually carried out with steam, but each producer subtly varies their own technique. In exposing the leaves to different steam conditions, producers have effectively created three principal styles of Sencha, each with its own distinct nuances.

THE ASAMUSHI STYLE

Produced with just a brief steaming (20 to 40 seconds), asamushi-style Sencha can be recognized by their complete and unbroken leaves. Often light and low in tannins, their taste is reminiscent of green vegetables and fresh grass.

THE FUKAMUSHI STYLE

The fukamushi style of Sencha is obtained with a longer steaming (80 to 200 seconds). Since the leaves are exposed for a longer period of time to the steam, they become more brittle and will break more easily. This leads to more intense flavour and a brisk, darker infusion.

THE CHUMUSHI STYLE

An intermediary zone separates the two styles of Sencha described above. Leaves that undergo a 40-to-80-second steaming belong to the chumushi style. These teas, which have a more typical Sencha flavour, are currently the most common on the Japanese market.

FIRING

The final firing, hiire, is an important process in green tea transformation. During this stage, the leaves are put in gas-heated cylinders, where they are dried at varying intensities. This firing, which takes place at the very end of the transformation process, can greatly influence the flavour of the tea. The principle is simple: the less you roast the leaves, the more you conserve vegetal, marine, and floral notes. Inversely, the longer the roasting process, the more the vegetal notes wane and make way for a roasty, nutty flavour, often compared to chicken broth.

Just a few decades ago, neither intensive roasting nor the fukamushi style were much appreciated. The Japanese green teas of that time conserved the traditional vegetal characteristic. The producers from the traditionalist Uji region remain the guardians of this style.

Today, however, in Japan and throughout the world, there is a growing interest amongst tea enthusiasts for the taste of roasted green teas. In addition to their tolerance of hotter and harder water, these teas' leaves give off more distinctly fruity aromas.

ROASTING

If leaves are exposed to several minutes of intense temperatures, around 200° C, a Hojicha or "roasted tea" is produced. This is a very popular tea found in Japanese restaurants. The roasting process softens the leaves' brisk and grassy character to make way for woody aromas and a light, caramelized sweetness. The result is a relaxing brew with gentle, digestive properties that make it an ideal tea to be served after a meal. Due to its full, rich flavor, Hojicha is greatly appreciated by chefs, who often make use of it in their cuisine. It pairs well with soy-seasoned dishes and is a perfect accompaniment for fish, particularly salmon. Many desserts are also flavoured with Hojicha.

THE CHALLENGE OF TEMOMICHA

In present-day Japan, the technique of manually kneading and rolling tea leaves to produce Temomicha is extremely rare. A mere one hundred producers are keeping this tradition alive. Seeking a reputation for excellence, only very small quantities are produced, all bound for annual regional and national competitions. Award-winning teas may sell from two to five thousand dollars per kilo, so it was a great privilege to be invited by Mr. Miyano to follow an intensive course on this unique technique, which he has been practicing for over a dozen years.

In his home, Mr. Miyano received us as old friends. As a welcoming tea, he prepared for us his latest, freshly-produced Temomicha. He then offered us work aprons with our names on them, which he had specially commissioned for the occasion.

Before beginning our training, our host cautioned us: with no breaks allowed during the seven-hour class, we had to be prepared. Armed with water bottles and our aprons, we entered the room where the leaf transformation was to take place. We were immediately struck by the heat in the studio: the temperature would reach up to 40° C over the course of the day. Not even questioning our capacity to stay focused for so long, Mr. Miyano got straight to the point explaining the numerous stages of the Temomicha transformation process.

Initially, our task appeared to be simple: using various rolling techniques, the leaves were to be fashioned into a pine needle shape. Easy enough, we thought.

And thanks to our teacher's clear explanations, the beginning stages did go very smoothly. First, we placed 1.2kg of fresh leaves on a gas-heated table and covered them with paper. In order to reduce the leaves' humidity content, we vigorously tossed and turned the leaves in the air with our fingers. We then used our hands to roll the tea leaves with precise and studied gestures to begin extracting their oils.

Following Mr. Miyano's very specific guidance, we tried hard to master the different rolling methods. The hands must be firm and the movements supple. With our focused gestures and the contact with the leaves, we gradually lost our sense of time, though the variety of different handling motions broke the monotony. As the hours went by, we became increasingly reverential of the nobility of this artisanal work, despite the laborious nature of the task.

The final stages were the hardest. The more one works the leaves, the more their water content evaporates, thus requiring ever more precise handling movements. With the leaves constantly drying out, the main difficulty in the transformation of a Temomicha is to conserve enough humidity in the leaves so that they don't break and can thus be crafted into the desired needle-shaped form.

Seven hours later, at the end of the class, we proudly compared our results with Mr. Miyano's and quickly realized that mastering this technique would definitely require a lot more experience.

INFUSION METHOD

To appreciate the full potential of a Temomicha by releasing its delicate floral aromas, its long finish, and slightly euphoric effect, it is preferable to use a shiboridashi, a small, flat porcelain or clay container. The long leaves of the tea are laid out lengthwise inside it in a triangular form.

Temomicha infusions require little water, which is heated at an exceptionally low temperature. The water is poured around the side of the stacked leaves so that they are infused from below.

MR. MIYANO'S INSTRUCTIONS
Place 4 to 5 grams of leaves in your shiboridashi or in a flat-bottom teapot.

1st infusion: 30 ml of water at 50° C for 1 1/2 minutes
2nd infusion: 30 ml of water at 60° C for 1 minute
3rd infusion: 50 ml of water at 70° C for 45 seconds
4th infusion: 100 ml of water at 75° C for 2 minutes

For each new infusion, be sure to transfer all of the liquid to another container to stop the leaves from over-steeping.

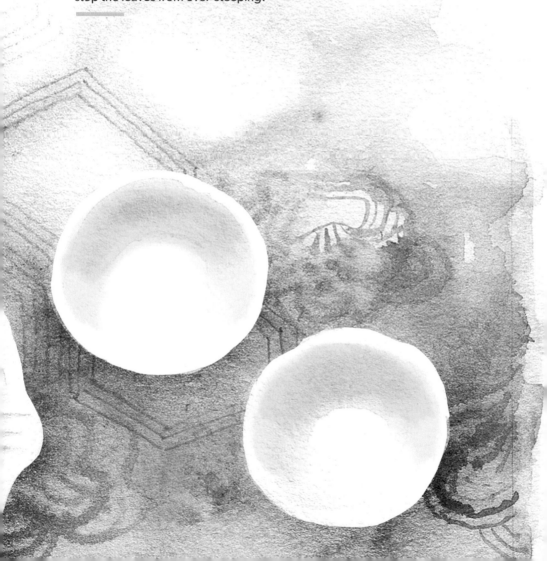

THE PLEASURE OF EATING
THE LEAVES

Given their fondness for fine cuisine, it is no surprise that the Japanese have developed a singular way to make the most of some teas' culinary qualities. Instead of throwing out the tea leaves, as is customary after several infusions, they put a small quantity of infused leaves on a plate, dress them with soy sauce or oil, and eat them as a salad.

Try this at home. The tender leaves of a shincha, high-quality Sencha, or Gyokuro are highly recommended.

YAMABUKI: A CULTIVAR WITH YELLOW LEAVES

In Japan, almost eighty percent of the cultivars used for green tea production are Yabukita. This cultivar was developed in the mid-1950s and has been prominent in Japanese plantations ever since. Its popularity amongst producers and consumers is due to its great adaptability to the climate of the archipelagos and to its lively, brisk flavour, which appeals to modern Japanese tastes.

Despite Yabukita's dominance as a cultivar, some Japanese producers, such as our friend Mr. Sugiyama, continually experiment with new cultivars alongside the old ones. With help from his father, Mr. Sugiyama has successfully diversified his plantations. His father has a passion for breeding plants and has experimented with the production and evaluation of new cultivars for over fifty years. Naturally, many of these tests yield unsatisfactory results, but every now and then a successful surprise will make all of the hard work worth the effort.

Several years ago, Mr. Sugiyama was astonished by the appearance of yellow leaves on a plant in his plantation. He believed these leaves were brought about by a series of natural genetic mutations. At the time, he did not expect that the tree with the yellow leaves would produce a quality tea, so the tree was transplanted close to his house as an ornamental plant.

A few years later, while working for the National Tea Laboratory of Japan, Mr. Sugiyama carried out a few experiments on the leaves of this tea tree and discovered that, when infused, the tea was both unusual and delicious. He decided to multiply this cultivar in a small section of his garden and named it Yamabuki, after a local flower with yellow petals.

According to Mr. Sugiyama, very few Japanese producers use cultivars similar to Yamabuki. He himself only produces a tiny quantity, five to ten kilos per year, and does not plan to increase production. This cultivar's leaves contain only one-fortieth of the chlorophyll contained in the common Yabukita cultivar. This difference considerably diminishes the trees' capacity to carry out the photo-synthesis essential for its growth. Fortunately, in the course of the season, its leaves do eventually become green as the plants are reinvigorated.

This unusual cultivar has only recently begun to attract attention in Japan. Just like Mr. Sugiyama, enthusiasts were not immediately won over by the yellow leaves, which they viewed as a flaw. Once the International Tea Com-petition of Japan took notice of its unusual taste, suggestive of asparagus, lamb's lettuce, and corn, however, it has now piqued the interest of a grow-ing number of tea lovers.

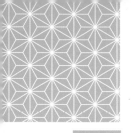

HAGI POTTERY

In 1592, Hideyoshi Toyotomi gathered an army of 160,000 warriors in the western region of Japan. His goal was to invade first Korea and then China. The Koreans put up little resistance, but the Chinese pressed the Japanese into retreat.

Though this invasion attempt failed, it had important repercussions on the city of Hagi, located on Honshu Island in Yamaguchi Prefecture. The soldiers brought back with them several hundred objects made by Korean master ceramists. During this time, many potters also emigrated from Korea to Japan, introducing their manufacturing and firing techniques to their new country. In Japan, the paternity of the Hagi pottery style is now attributed to Ri Shakko and Ri Kei, two brothers of Korean origin who were the first to produce works in this style on the Japanese archipelago.

Holding a Hagi bowl, one is instantly struck by the contrast between its chunky appearance and its light weight. This effect, typical of this pottery style, is due to a clay ventilation method that consists of mixing the clay with grog or sand. During the firing, the mixture creates minute deformations that add a distinct and unique feeling to each piece.

The milky glaze is another main feature of this style of ceramics. Its smoothness contrasts with the rough surface beneath. The glaze is visibly contracted, and the light crackling effect allows the tea to gradually permeate the pottery surface over time. In examining the bowl's base and its deep crazing, one can identify the clay that was used and make out how it reacted during firing.

Hagi pottery transforms and evolves over time, displaying a more personalized history of its use with every infusion. For the Japanese, the more one uses Hagi pottery, the more beautiful it becomes.

Tea enthusiasts generally use this type of pottery during the Japanese tea ceremony, but any tea can be enhanced by Hagi bowls.

AN INTERVIEW WITH MR. NAKAHARA, A POTTER FROM HAGI

Mr. Nakahara, how did you become a potter?

In Hagi, pottery is a local industry. Since I grew up in this city, I have always been close to this art. Many artisans lived close to my home. When the time came to choose a career, I naturally thought of becoming a potter.

Some Hagi pieces have a notch on their bottom. Why is that?

There was a period during which people were not authorized to use the same pottery as the emperor. To identify the bowls that were not intended for him, potters inscribed a notch. This tradition is still alive today.

In your opinion, what are the qualities of a good potter?

To begin with, to make good pottery, you must be skillful. You must have agile fingers. I believe that dexterity is a crucial part of pottery technique. You must also know how to use the potter's wheel. When I work, I think about pleasing my clients, about what format would be most useful for them, and so forth. The elegance and beauty of each piece are things I am very concerned about.

I also believe that one can sense an artist's humanity through his work. Analyzing a work of art is difficult for amateurs as well as professionals.

Even if they are not experts in pottery, most people feel something mysterious when they see or touch a piece. I believe that they can intuitively feel what kind of a person made the piece. So I think a good potter should have a positive outlook in his everyday life.

People say that the present-day Japanese have neither beliefs nor principles. I don't agree; I think that we all believe in something. Pottery is the mirror of an artist's way of life. I don't think that a buyer chooses my pieces randomly. I believe that you recognize me through my work.

How do you view the art of pottery in contemporary Japan, compared with the period when you began?

The pottery industry in Japan is very respectful of tradition. That being said, young potters have more difficulty if they don't come from a family of artisans who pass the torch from generation to generation. Maybe young artists are not given their fair due. Potters who have been established for a long time are highly respected by people in the industry. Their pottery is very expensive. This is how it was in the past and the situation has not changed.

TEA AND SHIITAKE

As in other fields, some innovations in the world of tea are purely due to chance. Without the acumen of keen producers, however, nothing would come of such accidental events. Mr. Iwata, a Japanese producer, strives constantly to improve the quality of his tea and recently discovered an unusual trick to enrich his garden's earth.

Mr. Iwata is very proud of his land, which has been cultivated by his family for seventeen generations. After so many lifetimes of organic agricultural practices, he still manages to improve his soil by adding compost and natural fertilizer. Watching him dig his hands into the earth to turn it over as he explains how he made his innovative discovery, the depth of his passion and love for his family's land is clear.

A great number of strawberry plants grow in the undergrowth between his gardens. In the summertime, Mr. Iwata enjoys collecting berries for his children. One day, after placing several bowls of strawberries on the table, he realized that his children had a preference for a particular batch of sweeter berries. Intrigued, he sought out the place where these tastier strawberries grew.

In the woods around the tea fields, much of the undergrowth was left wild, while other areas were used for shiitake growing. By comparing various strawberry patches, Mr. Iwata discovered that the sweeter berries came from earth around the logs he used to grow the mushrooms. Having become a part of the soil over the years, the decomposing logs used for shiitake growing turned out to be beneficial for the strawberries' flavour. This discovery left him wondering: could this trick also work for the tea plants?

To find out, Mr. Iwata decided to take advantage of this natural fertilizer and transported some of the shiitake-infused earth into his tea gardens. It is still too early to know how this will change the taste of the tea, but, according to Mr. Iwata, the advantage of this compost is that it provides the plants with a rich source of carbon and other necessary nutrients. He expects that the teas will be lighter, clearer, and sweeter. The next harvest may very well have some surprises in store.

———

SEARCHING FOR BALANCE

In most tea-producing countries, the majority of finished teas on the market are blends. These combinations are often created by mixing complimentary batches of leaves from different gardens or even from different regions.

In Japan, this standard blending practice is facilitated by the tea industry's set-up, which is divided into two main phases of production. The first phase brings the cultivation and manufacture stages together to create aracha ("raw product"); the second phase completes the transformation operation before the final sale.

Due to the high cost of equipment, few tea growers carry out all of the transformation stages. A grower's harvests are usually sold to specialized companies who transform the leaves into aracha. These companies then auction their products on the wholesale tea market. Other companies buy these lots of aracha to blend and transform them into a finished product. Those who carry out these assemblages are called chashi, a word that means "tea instructor," because they give instructions to the factory where the final transformation will take place.

The chashi tastes and chooses the lots according to the clients' criteria and the market demand. In mixing several harvests, he or she is able to make teas with a similar taste from one year to the next.

AN INTERVIEW WITH MR. OSADA,
A CHASHI AT MORI, SHIZUOKA

Mr. Osada, how did you begin your career as a tea instructor?

In the early 1990s, I realized that people were drinking increasingly less loose-leaf tea in this country. I therefore felt the need to get more involved and to participate in the development of tea culture. Around the same time, I heard about the new Association of Japanese Tea Instructors. I immediately registered for the course; I received my certification and became the association's first member.

What is the process behind the making of a blend?

First, I choose the tea lots based on their origin, transformation methods, and cultivars. After that, I study the product file, which provides information about the producer, harvest date, the grade of the leaves, and the number of available kilos. When I am interested in a lot, I infuse the leaves with boiling water to smell them. The boiling water reveals both the flaws and good qualities of the tea. In making a blend, I often start with a small amount of 100 grams. Once I obtain a satisfactory mix, I multiply the recipe to be applied to the number of kilos required.

Are there disadvantages to this practice?

No, provided you respect certain parameters. The principle is to maintain a balance between the taste, aroma, colour, and freshness. It is also important to consider the particular features of each tea lot: the characteristics of the terroir and the producers' distinctive trademarks. For example, mixing lots which all have strong aromas is not a good idea; too many strong aromas risk canceling each other out. To reach a balance, it is necessary to have a solid base flavour of the same intensity as the aromatics. Otherwise, one of these aspects will overwhelm the other.

What has this craft brought you?

Even though I have been working in the world of tea for thirty-three years, the arrival of the first spring harvests continues to fill me with a deep feeling of renewal. I believe that tea-growing tells us so much about human nature. I would like to thank all the artisans who are passionate about cultivating teas. I am also deeply grateful to my clients for the trust they have put in me.

THE ART OF MR. KAMADA

Mr. Kamada has been practicing the art of pottery for over forty years. He has dedicated the better part of his work to developing a modern and original vision of the Tenmoku style, which goes back to the Chinese Song dynasty [960-1279] and was introduced to Japan by Buddhist monks in the eighteenth century.

Mr. Kamada is one of the rare modern Japanese ceramists who have dedicated their life to creating pottery in the Tenmoku style and to researching its history. The fascinating glaze effects and the overall quality of his works have made him one of the most respected potters in Kyoto. His works are exhibited in many of Japan's most prestigious galleries. Since 2005, his most recent creations have also been part of the New York Metropolitan Museum of Art's permanent collection.

Upon meeting Mr. Kamada, we took the opportunity to ask him a few questions about his work, his methods, and the art of pottery.

AN INTERVIEW WITH MR. KAMADA, A POTTER FROM KYOTO

Mr. Kamada, after over forty years of practicing the craft, you have certainly developed a personal approach to pottery. What do you need to work?
I only need concentration and a suitable workspace.

What influences and motivates you in your work?
Before, I was inspired and influenced by the great tradition of ancient ceramic arts. I studied this subject, but reproducing this type of pottery is no longer a goal for me. Nowadays, I am more inspired by other forms of art or by nature. My main interest is to produce original works in the Tenmoku style. I get excited when a museum or the Japan Crafts Association invites me to exhibit my works. It is very stimulating to have this opportunity to show new works.

What does it take to be a good potter?

In my opinion, to always keep exploring is the best attitude. I learn a lot from my mistakes. For example, no matter how much I try to control the glazing, the effects are always different.

What is your view of the art of pottery in present-day Japan, in comparison with when you started?

When I began my career, there were many young potters and this art was very much alive. Since then, pottery has become quite diverse. Today, it is increasingly about design. It seems that the original character of a piece of pottery no longer has the same value. Consumers from all over the world can buy pottery without even touching the pieces. In an ideal world, I believe that people should have the opportunity to touch and hold the pieces before buying them.

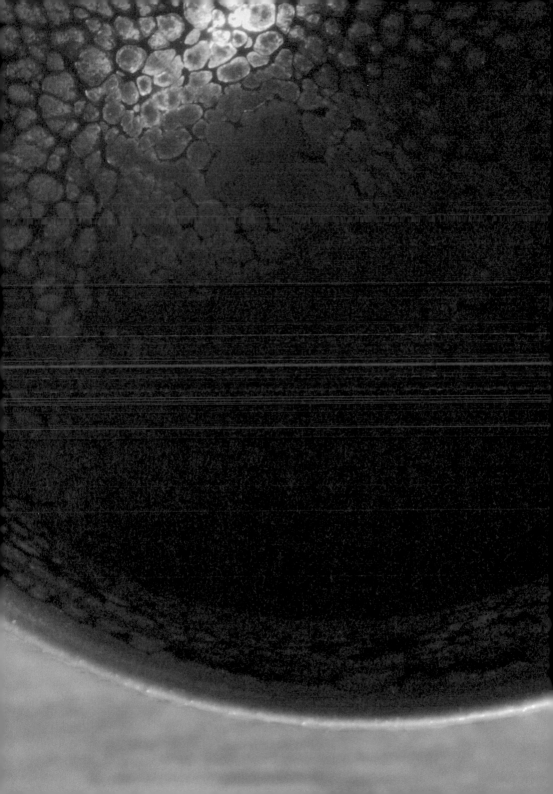

COVERED GROWING

From 1641 to 1853, Japan was isolated by the Sakoku Edict, which prohibited rela-tions with the world outside the archipelago. Japanese tea producers were cut off from China where they had been drawing their inspiration and now had to rely on their own imaginations. Kahei Yamamoto did just this in 1835 when he devised the covered growing process.

This process is unique in the world of tea. During the spring, a canopy is placed over the tea plants, which shades them and slows their growth. These canopies were traditionally made out of straw, but today they are of-ten made of modern mesh netting that reduces exposure to the sun from sixty to ninety-five percent.

The period of shade is usually divided into two cycles, each lasting about ten days. The first begins once the new, slow-growing shoots reach around two centimeters in height. This is followed by the second cycle during which the density of shade is increased until the tea plants are kept almost completely in the dark, retarding the growth even more.

Depriving the tea plants of light forces increased chlorophyll content. With diminished photosynthesis, nutrients drawn from the soil are not processed by the plants' typical systems, thus modifying the leaves' mo-lecular structure.

Deprived of light, the shoots grow slowly and are plucked later in the spring. To maximize the number of young shoots along the stem, the tea plants are not pruned. Despite the high cost of labour, pluckers must carefully clear each stem one at a time. The leaves of these shade-grown tea plants are used solely in premium-quality teas.

Used for Gyokuro, Kabusecha, Tencha, and Matcha, the covered growing cultivation technique generally produces teas with iodized aromas, full, sweet, vegetal notes, a rich liquor, and low astringency.

The Japanese have a high regard for teas that have been grown and transformed with such great care. This respect for high-quality leaves is expressed through very precise preparation and tasting techniques (see "Preparing Tea in a Senchado," pg. 164).

FRESHNESS AND GREEN TEA

Given their delicate floral fragrances, subtle notes of fresh-cut grass, and marine accents, green teas are best consumed fresh. The distinctive aromatic notes of spring teas tend to dissipate within months after the harvest.

To delay the natural aging of their green teas, the Japanese have shown great ingenuity. Depending on the market demand and quantities of tea produced in a specific year, they vacuum-pack a certain amount of aracha to be stored in enormous freezers. This keeps the aracha fresh until it is defrosted for processing.

Though Japan is perhaps the only country to freeze tea leaves on a large scale, many other tea-producing countries now use vacuum packaging. In China, the goal is not only to preserve the freshness of the teas, but also to sell tea in convenient units. Small 5g or 10g packets have become very popular with tea-drinkers, especially for Wulong teas. Some producers hesitate, however, as vacuum packaging, unless done very carefully, can break the more delicate leaves.

RULES FOR PRESERVING GREEN TEA AT HOME
1) The container must be airtight. Contact with the air encourages the aging of the leaves, causing the aromatic components to dissipate and the leaves' humidity, essential for a good infusion, to evaporate.

2) To prevent the colour of the leaves from fading and the taste from deteriorating, the tea must be kept away from light and heat. Glass containers should be avoided unless they are stored in a dark place.

3) Since tea tends to absorb odors, the containers must be kept far from fragrant foods, coffee, and spices.

WAGASHI

Thanks to the tradition passed down from generation to generation, the crafting of these little culinary gems has been refined for centuries. Today, they are a fully-integrated part of Japanese cuisine, a cuisine that strongly values beautiful presentation. Known as wagashi, these traditional Japanese pastries are a delight for the eyes, the palate, and the spirit.

Each region of Japan has developed its own wagashi style. Wagashi make a perfect compact snack for travelers, so pastry makers set up stands in many of the country's train stations. These popular stands sell common styles of regional wagashi.

To enhance their simple and poetic form, great care goes into wagashi presentation. Individually packed or in attractive assortment boxes, this diverse style of pastry comes in different shapes and sizes with names such as daifuku, dango, dorayaki, manjû, and youkan.

Other, more sophisticated wagashi are crafted to celebrate the beauty of nature. These kinds are often included in the Japanese tea ceremony. The form, colour, and flavours must be in harmony with the chosen theme. Created by master pastry chefs with their skilled hands, these small works of art are part of the aesthetic and gourmet pleasures linked to the ceremony.

Here we recommend two wagashi recipes that will be a perfect match for your favourite teas. The first is more traditional and requires time and patience. The second is more contemporary and easier to make.

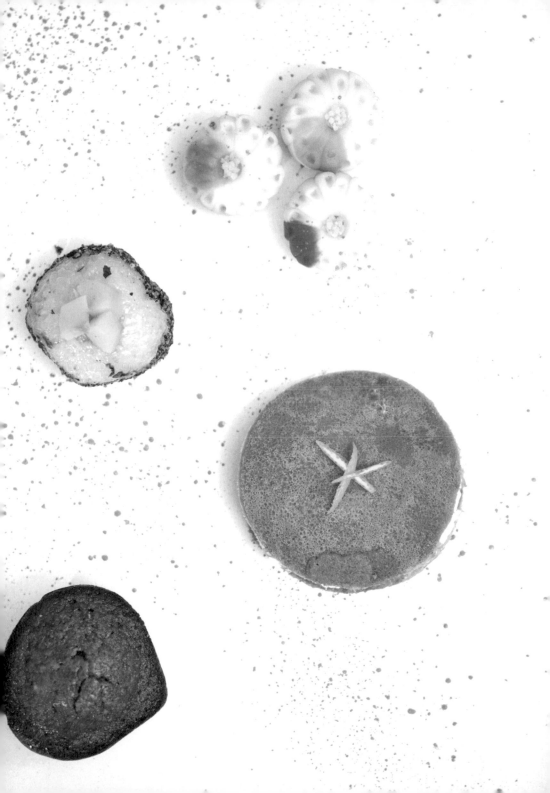

CHAKKURI MOCHI
(Makes 10 mochi)

1/2 cup (100g) sticky rice
1/2 cup (50 ml) water
1 tsp. Japanese Sencha green tea
2 Tbs. sugar
A pinch of salt
3 1/2 oz (100g) azuki paste[1] or azuki-anko
5 chestnuts, canned in syrup
Black sesame seeds or 10 red shiso leaves (for the garnish)

First, rinse the sticky rice and soak in 1 liter of water overnight. The next day, strain the rice and rub it between your hands to crush the grains.

Heat 1/4 cup water in a rice steamer and suspend a cloth over the steamer. Place prepared rice in cloth; cover and steam for 20 minutes. Set aside.

Prepare the tea infusion. In a small bowl, add 1/4 cup hot water (85° C). Add 1 teaspoon Sencha green tea and infuse for 5 minutes. Add tea infusion to rice. Mix together and let sit for about 1 hour.

Steam-cook the prepared rice for another 15 minutes, using the same cloth technique as above. Add sugar and salt. Mix again and let cool uncovered for 1 hour at room temperature.

To make the rice balls: wet hands, take a small quantity of rice, press a hole in the middle, insert a little azuki paste, and roll it into a ball. Quarter the chestnut and place a piece on top of each mochi ball.

For sesame seed garnish: place seeds in a bowl and dab the mochi into the seeds, covering the bottom half of the ball. For red shiso leaves garnish: wash and rinse leaves, sprinkle with salt, and let sit for 30 minutes. Rinse the leaves lightly so that only a slight taste of salt remains. Place the mochi on the leaf and fold around the sides until the mochi is half-covered.

---

1. You can either find azuki paste in specialized Asian grocery stores or you can make it yourself (see the recipe on pg. 115).

MATCHA CRÊPES WITH AZUKI WHIPPED CREAM
(Makes 8 crêpes)

Crêpes
1/8 cup (10 g) powdered green tea, such as Matcha Sora
1/2 cup (70 g) unbleached flour
1 Tbs. cornstarch
2 eggs
1/4 cup (45 g) sugar
1 cup (250 ml) milk
2 Tbs. unsalted butter, melted

Whipped cream
1/3 cup (70 ml) whipping cream
1/2 Tbs. sugar
1 3/4 oz (50 g) azuki paste[1] or azuki-anko

In a bowl, sift the green tea. Add flour and cornstarch; sift again. Make a hole in the middle of the mixture.

In another bowl, lightly whip eggs and sugar. Add milk and mix gently.

Slowly pour the wet mixture into the middle of the flour/tea mix. Stir lightly.

Add melted butter to the mixture and combine until an even consistency is obtained.

Stir mixture until smooth and let sit at room temperature for 1 hour.

Whip cream with sugar. Mix in the azuki paste. Place mixture in refrigerator for 10 minutes.

Using the prepared batter, cook small crêpes and let them cool. Place the whipped cream on the crêpes and fold in two.

---

1. You can either find azuki paste in specialized Asian grocery stores or you can make it yourself (see the recipe on pg. 116).

AZUKI PASTE

5 oz (150 g) dried azuki beans
3/4 cup (150 g) sugar
A pinch of salt

Boil beans in a large pot of water for 15 minutes. Drain, add new water, and cook beans at low heat for about 1 hour or until tender, making sure the beans are well immersed at all times. Drain well. Add sugar.

Continue cooking over low heat while stirring constantly until an even consistency is obtained. It is important to continue stirring, allowing water contained in the beans to evaporate.

Add salt. Let cool.

This mixture can be stored in the refrigerator for three days or in the freezer for three weeks.

THE BIRTH OF RAKU POTTERY

On February 28, 1591, having been sentenced to "death by suicide" by the powerful warrior General Hideyoshi, Sen No Rikyu organized a final ceremony with his followers. To ward off ill fortune before killing himself, he broke his tea bowl. Of an inestimable value, this bowl was said to have been made by the tile maker Chojiro, who, having followed Rikyu's specifications and standards, had become the originator of Raku pottery.

The bowl or chawan, an essential piece of the Japanese tea ceremony, grew to prominence in the sixteenth century due to its original design. Before that time, most chawan were made in China or Korea, but they were not specifically designed for this ceremony. When Sen No Rikyu reformed and codified the Japanese tea ceremony known as Chanoyu, the "Way of Tea," he was more interested in local pottery and sought simple, noble, and discreet objects for his image of this spiritual and aesthetic way of life.

Sen No Rikyu abandoned the perfection of porcelain for the simplicity of terracotta, which was more in keeping with the spirit of the tea ceremony. He commissioned a new type of bowl from Chojiro, a bowl that was to have a more cylindrical shape and inward-folded rims designed to conserve the tea's warmth during the winter season.

To respect Rikyu's specifications, Chojiro had to invent a new production technique. This led him to refine the tezukune method, which was inherited from the Koreans.

In the tezukune method, each chawan is handcrafted with sandstone grog. Layers are gradually raised around the sides of a base of this clay until the whole bowl is formed. The inside, outside, and base of the chawan are then shaped with a spatula. The glaze is applied before firing.

Chojiro's use of rapid firing was also revolutionary. This hikidashi method consists of putting a bowl into a hot kiln for several minutes, then removing it before the enamel vitrifies. Each bowl is fired individually and cooled at room temperature. Such rapid firing creates a porous ceramic with thick walls that are pleasant to the touch.

Chojiro succeeded in creating unique chawan of a rustic, imperfect nature free from the era's usual decorative elements and ideally suited for the tea ceremony. As a reward for his work, the shogun Taïko gave him a seal engraved with the ideogram "raku," evoking pleasure, joy, and spiritual gratification. From that point onward, Chojiro would use this seal on all of his pieces. Chojiro thus became the first in a long line of Japanese potters that have continued to uphold the essence of Raku pottery for over seventeen generations.

Today, the term Raku is applied to all ceramics created using this method, but production of this type of pottery is on the decline in Japan. In days gone by, Japanese wedding tradition called for each bride to bring a Raku chawan in her trousseau. The abandonment of this tradition has considerably reduced demand.

THE ROJI, A PASSAGEWAY

Roji is the name given to a path of natural stones that leads to the chashitsu, or tea-room. Before participating in a tea ceremony, guests walk down the roji that guides them through the different sections of the garden adjoining the chashitsu. Over the centuries, tea masters had developed various roji designs until Sen No Rikyu introduced a spiritual dimension.

Sen No Rikyu viewed the roji as a passageway, the final space to be crossed before entering the tearoom. The roji was therefore a preparatory stage for the tea ceremony, in which the spirit of tea prevails. A meditative experience marked by serenity, the passage through the roji was conceived as the transition between everyday life and the spiritual world. For Okakuro Kakuzo, the writer of the indispensable *Book of Tea*, "the roji was intended to break the connection with the outside world and to trigger a sensation of freshness conducive to the aesthetic enjoyment of the tearoom itself."

Towards the end of the sixteenth century, other tea masters, such as Furuta Oribe, brought a new dimension to the roji. In addition to creating optical effects that made the garden look bigger, Oribe divided the roji into two sections: the exterior roji (sotoroji) entrance area, and the interior roji (uchiroji). The door that separates the two sections symbolizes the border between the profane and sacred worlds.

Ideally, the tea garden should evoke the pure and simple beauty of nature. The guest who follows the roji to the chashitsu should have the impression of coming upon a humble cottage. Several elements serve to create this atmosphere.

TOBI-ISHI

The roji is paved with stones called tobi-ishi or "flying stones," which are arranged according to a very precise code. They serve to guide the guest's steps through the garden. Originally, they also made it possible for visitors to move through the garden without getting dirty. Today, their various forms and sizes naturally steer the guest. Small stones are used to slow down the visitors and focus their attention. Larger stones suggest suitable spots to pause and observe the garden's features. The layout of these stones thus paces and punctuates the walk to the chashitsu. During hot summer days, water may be poured onto these stones to refresh the garden.

TSUKUBAI

Another essential roji element, the tsukubai is a basin for the ritual cleansing that precedes the tea ceremony. At this point, one cleanses both hands and mouth. Set deliberately at ground level, the tsukubai obliges visitors to bend down. A bamboo ladle is placed on the basin's edge. Every stone around the tsukubai has a specific significance according to its location.

TÔRÔ

The tôrô are stone lanterns used for evening ceremonies. They are both practical and aesthetic. Located near the tsukubai and chashitsu, they illuminate the visitor's way. In Sen No Rikyu's view, this song holds the secret to building a roji.

I looked beyond:
no flowers
and no colourful leaves.
At the path's end, a lone cabin stands
in the dying light
of an autumn evening.

The design of a roji encourages visitors to become aware of themselves and their surroundings. In leading them to "look beyond," the roji makes it possible to forget everyday worries and to attain the serenity required for the tea ceremony.

A SAMURAI'S LAST MATCHA

Imagine that you are a seventeenth-century samurai. On the orders of your ruler, you must fight in a losing battle. There is one thing you must do before taking up arms: walk down the roji until you reach the chashitsu, where your last bowl of tea awaits you.

The chashitsu is built out of the way at the end of the garden. You notice the clean path, the freshly watered-down stones, the garden's colourful flowers. The path leads to the tsukubai, the stone basin. You cleanse your mouth and hands with the fresh water.

The host is ready to receive you in the tearoom. The low, narrow door gives you no choice but to leave your sword outside. This is the only place where you allow yourself to be disarmed. For the ceremony, a small fan attached to your belt symbolizes your sword.

The light inside the chashitsu is subdued: a mild incense fragrance floats in the air, and water is heating up in the kama. You move towards the tokono-ma to read the poem written in calligraphy. The flowers are beautiful. You kneel to take your seat.

The ceremony's theme has been wisely chosen by the host, who sits serenely on the tatami. You are deeply concentrating and your senses are alert.

His first gestures are precise and admirable. The perfectly arranged utensils are simple, noble, and beautiful. He handles them with respect, purifying and placing them harmoniously. He puts two spoonfuls of green tea powder in the heated bowl. Then, with a more sweeping motion, he draws water from the kama, pours it over the tea, picks up the chasen, and whisks the tea for a few seconds, until he obtains a jade-coloured foam.

The host puts the bowl before you. You wait a moment before taking it. The tea is a gleaming green, conjuring up an image of glistening grass after a rainfall. Hypnotized by this colour, you let go, your mind free.

Time stands still. Outside, war is no longer. Your life appears to you like a pure, straight line.

You take the bowl with confidence, placing it in your left hand. You turn it halfway around and slowly draw it close to your lips. The first sip surprises you like a whiplash: the liquid is smooth and its bitterness illuminates your mind. The following sip, which is mild and tasty, comforts you in an unexpected way. You enjoy it calmly. The third sip is a sublime pleasure. You are overcome by a pleasant feeling of lightness.

And as your lips touch the bowl for the last time, the ground outside trembles.

You contemplate the bowl and the utensils, absorb the poem on the wall. You bid your host farewell and return outside, your senses still alert and your mind now at peace.

和敬清寂

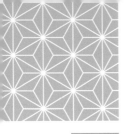

AN INTERVIEW WITH
A TEA CEREMONY INITIATE

RICHARD CHAPDELAINE,
A STUDENT OF KAGEMORI-SENSEI AT THE URASENKE SCHOOL

In Japan, several schools teach the tea ceremony and there are many students. In the West, there are not as many people practicing it at an advanced level. What led you to study and practice the tea ceremony?

Before I knew this ceremony, I practiced karate and was interested in haikus and ikebana (flower arrangement). I had a fascination with Japanese art and culture. In 1989, a friend introduced me to Kagemori-sensei from the Urasenke school and I immediately fell in love with the Chanoyu: the gestures, aesthetics, and basic principles of the "Way of Tea." I had found a world that suited me perfectly.

You have been practicing the Japanese tea ceremony for over twenty years. Have you ever come up against any difficulties?

In Japanese culture, the apprenticeship of an art is passed down "from one soul to another," which is to say that the master should lead us to discover a gesture or a nuance on our own, rather than whispering the solution directly in one's ear. The information is thus imprinted in our mind.

For a Westerner, the "why" of each thing is paramount, but for the Japanese, respect and trust are also understood between the lines. The stages are linked, one after the other. This is the "Way of Tea."

As for the manipulations, the most complex ones involve small objects—for instance, the chashaku. Toyotomi Hideyoshi stated, "Whoever can properly manipulate a chashaku in a tea room will also be able to handle a sword." It is the nuances within the gestures that are difficult to acquire.

In the first years, I practiced twice a day: at five o'clock in the morning before beginning my day, and in the evening before going to sleep. Now I carry out the tea ceremony every day, but the philosophy has become more internalized. I am less stressed. I do not dwell on error. The "Way of Tea" is now part of my life.

The Japanese say that there are as many different procedures for the ceremony as there are reasons to get together over a cup of tea.
This is true, but I didn't orient my apprenticeship around a specific procedure. When I receive guests, my only pleasure consists of offering a bowl of tea while respecting the basic principles in the best way possible. Nothing is left to chance: the decoration of the alcove, the choice of pottery, the style of procedure, the thousand-and-one details to look after before the guests' arrival. By virtue of the four basic principles— Harmony, Respect, Purity, and Tranquility—they will experience this unique moment.

Has this passion for the "Way of Tea" had an impact on your every-day life?
Thanks to this discipline, I learned how to focus on what I am doing and not what I will be doing. One of the notions of the "Way of Tea" is learning how to stop. One must learn how to be mindful of everything one does, in every detail and at every moment. "Tomorrow is another day," as they say in Japan. The most important thing is what is happening in the here and now.

OTHER PERSPECTIVES

The cultivation and consumption of green tea is wide-spread throughout Asia. Although the influences of Chinese and Japanese tea practices are ever-present, other countries have made green tea part of their own culture by adopting manufacturing techniques that correspond to their native plants, tastes, and market demand.

TEA IN THE STREETS OF VIETNAM

Hundreds of tea stands are set up on street corners close to busy intersections, preparing tea for passersby. From morning to evening, for about fifteen cents per glass, local workers take their breaks here, sitting on plastic benches and drinking their tea before heading back to their jobs.

It is at one of these intersections in the capital city of Hanoi that Ms. Thìn and her mother run a small tea stand. Every day, rain or shine, they share the work in shifts. At five o'clock in the morning, her mother readies the stand for their first clients, who are often homebound nightshift workers. Around 10 am, Ms. Thìn takes over until closing time in the early evening.

The green tea offered at these tea stands is made out of twisted whole leaves. Ms. Thìn prepares the tea by using a free-leaf, unfiltered infusion, allowing the leaves to expand at the bottom of the teapot in order to extract all of their potential flavour. Though she occasionally adds hot water to the leaves before changing them, the result is a relatively strong and bitter tea, the style most loved by the Vietnamese. Throughout the day the full kettle is placed on a propane gas burner, where it remains hot and ready for the next infusion.

In Vietnam, these small businesses hold an important social function. They are a place to discuss daily news or gossip, share one's interests, or to simply relax in good company. For Ms. Thìn, what matters most is that her clients enjoy her tea and know how to appreciate it. She tells us that it makes her happy when people talk about the colour and taste of her infusions.

According to Ms. Thìn, the quality of the water is perhaps the most crucial element in preparing a good tea. Her secret is to let the water sit all night in earthenware jars. During the day Ms. Thìn has a trusty assistant who goes back and forth between her house and the stand carrying the water for her infusions.

CHÈ Thìn

Thơm Ngon Đặc Biệt

25 HÀNG THAN   ĐT : 9271920

To stock up on tea, she goes directly to the producers in Thai Nguyen, where the tea is usually chosen by smelling and chewing the leaves. She admits that she finds it quite difficult to make these purchases. The ability to identify the strengths and flaws of teas in order to make a good selection requires much experience. She prefers preparing the tea at her stand.

Looking to the future, Ms. Thìn is more reserved. An increasing number of buildings are being bought by big stores and she worries that there will be less and less sidewalk space for her tea stand. Hearing this, a client inter-

jects and says that if things continue to progress as slowly as they are in the rest of Vietnam, Ms. Thìn (pictured below) is safe for another hundred years.

Thanking her for her time, we wish her happiness and prosperity and continue on our way.

TEA IN WOMEN'S HANDS

Though many women participate in tea harvesting activities, they are not as present in the tasks involved in tea manufacture, most of which are traditionally and still carried out by men. There are exceptions, however. In Vietnam's Thai Nguyen region, it is mostly women taking care of tea production, from the first cultivation to the final sales.

According to Ms. Hiep, the inspiring 67-year-old manager of the Tan Huong Cooperative, the dominant role women play in her company reflects the reality throughout Vietnam, where women occupy eighty percent of all jobs in the tea domain. Amongst this small cooperative's thirty-seven employees, only five are men. Sharing all of the tasks and equipment, men and women jointly produce a green tea comprised of large twisted leaves intended for the domestic market.

Despite the quality of the teas produced in Thai Nguyen, Vietnam's most renowned tea region, the market is quite saturated. Some growers limit their production to avoid a surplus. In seeking to develop Vietnam's primarily domestically-oriented tea market, some artisans have attempted to produce small-leaf teas of a higher quality; sadly, due to a lack of regular buyers, they are usually forced to return to their regular production.

This market reality, common to many tea regions, has forced some growers to develop new lines of traditional and everyday teas. Over the last few years, the Tan Huong Cooperative has been making Wulong tea in an attempt to diversify their production. On international markets, Wulong can sell for up to four times the price of their regular green tea and demand is on the rise. Should the cooperative succeed in introducing this new tea to the international market, it will certainly have a great positive impact.

With this in mind, in 1997, the women from Tan Huong began to plant the cultivars used to produce Wulongs. Without the expertise or equipment

required to transform these leaves, however, they have not yet managed to develop a satisfactory product. To address this problem, the cooperative has recently joined ranks with Mr. Xu, a Taiwanese specialist, to learn more about Wulong transformation processes and the complexity of parameters that must be respected to create a quality tea.

According to Ms. Hiep (pictured below), their recent progress has been very encouraging, but, before entering the foreign market, the cooperative will have to resolve many other organizational challenges regarding transportation, financial transactions, and quality control. With Mr. Xu's help, the members' perseverance, and the good fortune of having the support of the next generation ready to join them, the future looks bright for the Tan Huong Cooperative.

SNOW MOUNTAIN

Green tea production in Vietnam has little diversity. The primarily low-end produc-
tion is reserved for the domestic market. To track down some original, premium,
local production, we asked artisans and others working in the tea industry for rec-
ommendations. During these conversations, one name was mentioned repeatedly:
Tuyet San, "Snow Mountain."

According to some sources, Tuyet San tea has to be produced with the
leaves of old tea plants. At first this led us to believe that the tea in ques-
tion was a Pu-erh, the style that typically uses leaves from old tea plants to
produce premium teas. Curious to discover the transformation techniques
of the remote northwestern region of Vietnam and unearth a new Pu-erh
terroir, we set off in that direction.

After a long day's travelling from Hanoi, we arrived in a small village on
the plantation of Mr. and Ms. Hai, the location sitting at an altitude of over
1,300 meters. The majestic trees, randomly spaced here and there over the
slopes, are reputed to be between a hundred to three hundred years old.
Fully aware of the value of this plantation, Mr. Hai intends to ensure that it is
conserved in its natural state.

When Ms. Hai showed us her Tuyet San tea, we were very surprised to be
shown a green tea and not the maocha—a Pu-erh in leaf form—that we were
expecting. Tuning in to our pursuit of quality, she presented us with her highest grade of tea, of which the Hai family can only produce several kilos a year.

This grade is made up solely of buds, which gives it the appearance of a
white tea. Its mild and aromatic infusion reveals the qualities of the old tea
trees from which it originates, the rich flavor profile of trees drawing from

expansive root systems. The resulting impression is that of tasting the essence of the tree, quite an exceptional flavour characteristic for a green tea. While deeply appreciating the delicious tasting notes of Tuyet San, we contemplated the leave's potential to create an excellent and original Pu-erh -style aged tea.

INDIAN GREEN TEAS FROM KANGRA

To meet the needs of the West, the tea industry developed by the British during the nineteenth century in India specialized in black tea production. Famed regions such as Darjeeling, Assam, and Nilgiri emerged over the course of time, while other, more obscure regions such as Kangra are still trying to position themselves on the international market.

In 1849, the first Chinese tea seeds arrived in the Himalayan region of Kangra in the state of Himachal Pradesh. Over the following decades, a small tea industry developed. The rich soil, an ideal climate for tea cultivation, and the tea gardens' advantageous altitude at 1500 meters made this a favorable terroir similar to that of Darjeeling.

Unlike the Assam and Darjeeling regions, however, which rapidly dominated the export market, the Kangra region focused on producing teas for the domestic and regional market. In 1900, it was mainly dedicated to the production of green tea, most of which was shipped through the market city of Amritsar to the trade routes of Kashmir, Pakistan, and Afghanistan. At the height of production during the first half of the twentieth century, Kangra also exported its tea to North Africa, where green tea with mint was a popular beverage.

Today all that remains in Kangra is a fragile industry. After a series of natural and human catastrophes—epidemics, earthquakes, and repeated market declines—Kangra now survives on a small amount of green tea production for the Kashmir market and low-grade black tea production for the auctions in Calcutta. The loss of the Afghan market, due to war and the abundance of teas exported from Assam, Vietnam, and other Asian regions, has weakened this industry even further.

The Kangra producers are going through particularly difficult times. In spite of the remarkable plant wealth and an environment well suited for the development of distinctive teas, several decades without commercial success, coupled with diminishing interest in the industry, have contributed to Kangra's waning success. For many producers, the plants that make up their gardens are a burden rather than a valuable form of heritage. Presently, forty percent of the tea gardens in Kangra are in a state of neglect or are completely abandoned.

During a recent trip, however, we did observe the early signs of a potential rebirth. Some optimistic growers have begun to produce small quantities of high-quality teas, thus drawing attention to the potential of this Indian terroir. Moreover, Kangra is now part of the four Indian regions, along with Nilgiri, Assam, and Darjeeling, that have internationally recognized Geographical Indications. This will hopefully contribute towards boosting the popularity of Kangra teas in the coming years.

In India, it is customary to drink tea with spices (masala chai). Contrary to other regions in India where tea, known as chai, is made with black tea, in the Kangra region it is prepared with green tea.

KAHWA

Green tea prepared this way creates a clear tea with a golden, refreshing liquor and subtle notes of spice. In India, Kahwa is often reserved for special occasion or religious festivals.

4 cups (1 liter) water
2 green cardamom pods
1 cinnamon stick
2 cloves
4 Tbs. of strong green tea
A pinch of saffron
Sugar or honey
8 blanched and cut almonds

Add the cardamom, cinnamon, and cloves to the water and bring to a boil, then let simmer for 5 to 10 minutes. Modify the quantity of spices according to taste.

Add the tea leaves and simmer for 4 to 5 more minutes.

In another bowl, infuse the saffron in 1/2 cup (100 ml) of warm water for a few minutes.

Filter the preparation containing the tea leaves. Add the saffron infusion.

Sweeten to taste.

Serve hot in small cups with almond pieces.

Rose petals are sometimes added to liven up the tea with an extra aromatic touch.

GULAB CHAI

Gulab Chai is a warm and comforting drink, perfect for the harsh winter months in the mountains. It resembles the traditional chai that is consumed throughout India and made with milk or a thick, lumpy cream. Although Gulab Chai is often seasoned with salt, one can also use sugar or honey.

3 cups (750 ml) water
4 Tbs. strong green tea
1/2 Tbs. baking soda
3 green cardamom pods
2 star anise
2 cups (500 ml) milk
2 Tbs. pistachios
Sugar, honey, or salt

In a pot, bring water to a boil. Add the tea and baking soda and simmer for 20 to 25 minutes

Add cardamom and star anise. Let boil another 5 to 10 minutes.

Use a sifter to pour the liquid into another pot and add 1 cup (250 ml) of cold water.

Rapidly bring to a boil as you add milk and pistachios, all the while beating the tea into a frothy consistency. Add sugar, honey, or salt to taste.

TEA MATTERS

Tea sharpens and clears the mind, eases all tensions—be they mental or physical—and promotes a calm so deep that all the worries and troubles of everyday life are dispelled for a while.

Emperor Huizong [1082-1135]

GREEN PROPERTIES

The current surge of green tea's popularity in the West has allowed a new market of tea drinkers to discover a world of flavours and properties that the people of Asia have enjoyed for centuries.

Recent clinical studies confirm green tea's abilities to fight fatigue, reduce hypertension, support the cardiovascular system, stimulate blood flow, lower the chance of heart disease, help eliminate toxins, boost the immune system, promote good digestion, and provide a wide array of other health benefits. Due to its significant polyphenol content, its antioxidant properties are also known to reduce the risk of certain forms of cancer. Green tea provides a vast multitude of benefits for those who include it as part of their daily diet.

ANTIOXIDANT POWER

Antioxidants, which are found naturally in many foods, can help neutralize some of an organism's free radicals, the instable molecules that stabilize by binding with other molecules of the metabolism. This phenomenon alters and deteriorates the healthy molecules. All organisms have a certain reserve of antioxidant molecules that counteract the effect of the free radicals by neutralizing them. Unfortunately, this reserve is not always sufficient. A regular intake of foods that are rich in antioxidants can thus prevent or delay the damage free radicals cause to the cells and tissues of the human body.

The anti-cancer and protective properties attributed to tea are for the most part due to the presence of a subclass of polyphenolic molecules called catechins. These antioxidant compounds are secondary metabolites that play a defensive role for the plant. Of all the catechins in existence, the one with the strongest antioxidant effect is epigallocatechin gallate (EGCG), a high concentration of which is found in tea.

To evaluate the antioxidant power of each tea, ABTS/TEAC[1]—a screening method that allows researchers to compare several samples of the same nature—was used.

---

1. ABTS: a chemical compound used to evaluate the antioxidant capacity of a food. TEAC (Trolox Equivalent Antioxydant Capacity): a measure of the antioxidant capacity of a given substance, as compared to the standard, Trolox, an equivalent that is soluble in vitamin E liquid.

Though it is difficult to determine a food's antioxidant capacity on the basis of a sole analysis, this method makes it possible to reproduce the various free radical trapping mechanisms found in the human body. It also provides an overall picture of tea's capacity to prevent a variety of diseases associated with the presence of free radicals in humans.

CAFFEINE

Caffeine is an alkaloid that acts as a stimulant. It is found in numerous natural products such as coffee, yerba mate, guarana, and cacao.

Recognized since 1838 as being identical to the caffeine in coffee, the caffeine in tea—sometimes referred to as theine—bonds differently with its other elements. During a tea infusion, this alkaloid binds with tannins, attenuating and regularizing its effect. Even when a cup of tea contains more caffeine than a cup of coffee, it will have a longer, smoother, less aggressive rate of absorption that also lasts much longer. While caffeine acts primarily on blood flow by accelerating the heartbeat, the caffeine in tea mainly stimulates the cardiovascular system by dilating the blood vessels of the cerebral cortex.

While coffee is a short-term stimulant, tea energizes over the long-term. Tea sharpens the mind, heightens concentration and reflex capacity, keeps you alert, and boosts intellectual performance.

BIOCHEMICAL ANALYSIS RESULTS

To follow up on the data published in our first book, Tea: History, Terroirs, Varieties, *we continued our research on the antioxidant power and caffeine concentration of twenty-five new green teas.*

Our applied research protocols enabled us to indicate the exact amount that an infused tea contains based on the chosen preparation method. The leaves of each tea were infused in a porcelain teapot at 5 g for 500 ml of water. The data was compiled while the teas were hot, i.e. after the recommended infusion time and as soon as the liquid was transferred to another teapot. Thus we tested tea that was in the same state that we actually drink it at home. For Matcha (powdered tea), the analyses were carried out with 1.5 g of tea mixed with 100 ml of water. All of the analyzed teas were infused with spring water.

ANTIOXIDANT CONCENTRATION[1]

The loose-leaf teas were infused at 5 g of tea per 500 ml of water.

Teas	Country of Production	Water Temperature	Duration of Infusion	Concentration of TEAC (.moles / 250 ml)
Sencha Mobata	Japan	75° C	3.5 min	3410
Dong Shan	China	85° C	3.5 min	3180
Sencha Yamabuki	Japan	75° C	3.5 min	3015
Sencha Haruno	Japan	75° C	3.5 min	2770
Zhu Ye Qing	China	85° C	3.5 min	2735
Lu An Gua Pian	China	85° C	4.0 min	2500
Guricha	Japan	80° C	3.5 min	2490
Tan Huong	Vietnam	85° C	3.5 min	2435
Sencha Nagashima	Japan	75° C	3.5 min	2280
Sencha Tsuyu Hikari	Japan	70° C	3.5 min	2215
Long Jing Shi Feng	China	80° C	4.5 min	2200
Bi Luo Chun	China	80° C	3.5 min	2105
Anji Bai Cha	China	85° C	6.0 min	1800
Huo Shan Huang Ya	China	80° C	4.5 min	1785
Tai Ping Hou Kui	China	85° C	6.0 min	1750
Lu Shan Yun Wu	China	80° C	4.5 min	1665

Teas	Country of Production	Water Temperature	Duration of Infusion	Concentration of TEAC (.moles / 250 ml)
Gyokuro Hokuen	Japan	70° C	3.5 min	1535
Huiming Bai Ye	China	85° C	4.0 min	1530
Lan Xiang	China	85° C	4.5 min	1450
Huang Shan Mao Feng	China	80° C	4.5 min	1310
Kamairicha	Japan	80° C	3.5 min	1275
Gyokuro Shuin	Japan	70" C	3.5 min	1255
Bocha	Japan	80° C	3.5 min	1150
Bancha Shizuoka	Japan	85° C	4.5 min	1075
Bai Mu Dan (white)	China	80° C	6.0 min	1025
Xue Ya	China	85° C	5.5 min	950
Sencha Ashikubo	Japan	75° C	3.5 min	900
Xin Yang Mao Jian	China	80° C	3.5 min	700
Bai Hao Yin Zhen (white)	China	75° C	6.0 min	700
Sencha Tsukigase	Japan	75° C	3.5 min	575
Huiming	China	85° C	4.5 min	500
Gyokuro Tamahomare	Japan	65° C	4.5 min	375
Sencha Fukamushi Aji	Japan	75° C	3.5 min	350
Dragon Pearls (jasmine)	China	85° C	3.5 min	175

The matcha teas were whisked in a bowl at 1.5 g per 100 ml of water.

Teas	Country of Production	Water Temperature	Duration of Infusion	.moles / 100 ml
Matcha Suisen	Japan	70° C	30 sec	1808
Matcha Sendo	Japan	70° C	30 sec	1510
Matcha Uji	Japan	70° C	30 sec	1486
Matcha Asahi	Japan	70° C	30 sec	1406
Matcha Choan	Japan	70° C	30 sec	1212

---

1. Measured using the ABTS-TEAC method.

CAFFEINE CONCENTRATION[1]

The teas were infused at 5 g of tea per 500 ml of water.

Teas	Country of Production	Water Temperature	Duration of Infusion	Caffeine (mg / 250 ml)
Dong Shan	China	85° C	3.5 min	62
Gyokuro Shuin	Japan	70° C	3.5 min	61
Lu An Gua Pian	China	80° C	4.5 min	60
Tai Ping Hou Kui	China	85° C	6.0 min	59
Kamairicha	Japan	80° C	3.5 min	59
Lan Xiang	China	85° C	4.5 min	58
Wei Shan Mao Jian	China	85° C	3.5 min	58
Wuyuan Zi Mei	China	85° C	3.5 min	58
Sencha Tsuyu Hikari	Japan	70° C	3.5 min	58
Tan Huong	Vietnam	85° C	3.5 min	56
Zhu Ye Qing	China	85° C	3.5 min	55
Bi Luo Chun	China	80° C	3.5 min	53
Sencha Mobata	Japan	75° C	3.5 min	51
Xue Ya	China	85° C	5.5 min	50
Sencha Ashikubo	Japan	75° C	4.5 min	48
Long Jing Shi Feng	China	85° C	4.5 min	48
Guricha	Japan	80° C	3.5 min	45
Gyokuro Hokuen	Japan	70° C	3.5 min	45
Sencha Haruno	Japan	75° C	3.5 min	41
Bai Mu Dan (white)	China	80° C	6.0 min	39
Sencha Nagashima	Japan	75° C	3.5 min	37
Hojicha Shizuoka	Japan	95° C	4.5 min	27
Bancha Shizuoka	Japan	85° C	4.5 min	18
Bocha	Japan	80° C	3.5 min	17
Bai Hao Yin Zhen (white)	China	75° C	6.0 min	15
Gyokuro Tamahomare	Japan	65° C	4.5 min	14
Sencha Fukamushi Aji	Japan	75° C	4.5 min	14
Huiming	China	85° C	4.5 min	13
Dragon Pearls (jasmine)	China	85° C	3.5 min	13

1. Measured using liquid UV chromatography.

The matcha teas were whisked in a bowl at 1.5 g per 100 ml of water.

Teas	Country of Production	Water Temperature	Duration of Infusion	Caffeine (mg / 100 ml)
Matcha Choan	Japan	70° C	30 sec	51
Matcha Sendo	Japan	70° C	30 sec	50
Matcha Uji	Japan	70° C	30 sec	47
Matcha Asahi	Japan	70° C	30 sec	44
Matcha Suisen	Japan	70° C	30 sec	42

ICED TEA AND CAFFEINE

With the growing popularity of iced tea, we also tested how preparation methods influenced their caffeine content. To obtain the best flavour for iced teas, we often recommend infusing leaves for up to 12 hours in cold water, so we analyzed an infusion of 7.5 g of tea in 750 ml of cold water for 12 hours and compared it with a hot water infusion. The latter, also prepared with 7.5 g of leaves, was in 325 ml of hot water for 3.5 minutes before being cooled down with an equivalent quantity of ice, after which the analyses were carried out.

Both teas were infused at 7.5 g of tea per 750 ml of water.

Teas	Country of Production	Water Temperature	Duration of Infusion	Caffeine (mg / 250 ml)
Long Jing iced tea (hot infusion)	China	85° C	3.5 min	37
Long Jing iced tea (cold infusion)	China	4° C	12 hr	26

INTERPRETATION OF THE RESULTS

Thanks to our new laboratory studies of over seventy different teas, we now have a better understanding of the factors that influence tea's caffeine and antioxidant concentration. After putting these results together, we are presented with several possible interpretations.

In our studies, leaves that had been more heavily heat-treated had reduced antioxidant content. We noticed that teas that had undergone a longer steaming or initial firing had smaller antioxidant concentrations than those which had undergone a short steaming or initial firing. Thus, a long steaming may alter the quantity or release of certain chemical compounds in the leaves.

The maturity of the plant material may also have an influence on the caffeine and antioxidant content. Leaves plucked in more mature phases of growth tended towards higher concentrations. Most of the teas showing high concentrations were made from larger leaves, adding weight to this hypothesis.

We also noticed a correlation between the caffeine content and the antioxidant content, with most of the teas with high caffeine content also having high concentrations of antioxidants.

Before drawing definitive conclusions, however, there is still much work to be done. If we account for all of the diverse variables involved in tea's cultivation and manufacture, there is a significant amount of data still to be gathered. In order to provide tea enthusiasts with more complete and accurate details on the many benefits of tea, we must dedicate ourselves to further scientific research and laboratory studies.

WATER, TEA, AND TIME

"The 'Way of Tea' is nothing but this: first you boil water, then you make the tea and drink it accordingly." Sen No Rikyu aptly summarizes here the simplicity to be attained in tea practice. But how can one assist tea in releasing its full potential? How can its hidden subtleties be revealed?

The art of tea preparation is primarily about mastering the infusion technique. Several parameters must be taken into account: the quality of the water and the tea, the ratio of water per quantity of leaf, the temperature of the water, and the duration of infusion. Once one understands the relationship between these different factors, preparing tea becomes less of a conscious activity and more of an intuitive one.

Composed of delicate buds and tender shoots, green teas are often quite fragile. Boiling water can rapidly modify these leaves and damage their precious aromas; an over-extended infusion can even push their brisk, lively characteristics into bitterness. As a general rule, for a successful infusion, one uses one teaspoon or 2.5 g of tea leaves per cup, simmers the water at 70 to 85° C, and employs an infusion duration of 3 to 5 minutes.

Diverse techniques make it possible to vary the approach to preparation and to discover many different facets of the same tea. The following tables present the infusion parameters for the principal styles of green tea.

PREPARING TEA IN A TEAPOT

1. Heat the teapot for a few seconds by pouring hot water into it and then emptying the pot.

2. Place the leaves into a filter or directly into the teapot.

Infusion in a Teapot	Amount per Cup (250 ml)	Temperature	Duration of Infusion	Notes
Small-leaf Chinese green tea	1 tsp. (2.5 g)	75 to 85° C	3 to 5 min	The higher the quality of the tea and the higher its bud content, the lower the water temperature should be.
Large-leaf Chinese green tea	1 ½ tsp. (3 g)	75 to 85° C	4 to 5 min	
Japanese green tea	1 tsp. (2.5 g)	65 to 80° C	3 to 4 min	For high-quality Gyokuro and Sencha, it is preferable to infuse the tea at 65° C.

3. Pour the water at the right temperature over the leaves. Let it infuse for the desired time.

4. Remove the filter or transfer the liquid to another vessel. Enjoy.

CONCENTRATING THE FLAVOURS

Following the saying "the smaller the teapot, the better the tea," China and Japan have each developed a method to optimize the taste of green teas.

Though the basic principle is the same, other infusion techniques use short infusions with a large quantity of leaves and a small volume of water to concentrate the flavours. In addition to accentuating the taste of the tea and revealing more subtle nuances with each infusion, these methods encourage variation, invention, and the freedom to adapt the tea infusion to one's taste. Whereas the Chinese use the gaiwan technique, the Japanese equivalent is called Senchado.

CHINESE TECHNIQUE

The gaiwan, or zhong, is the preferred utensil for the infusion of Chinese green teas. It has been used in China since the end of the Ming dynasty [1368-1644], and even though it is no longer as popular as it once was for green tea infusion, it is still commonly used by many tea enthusiasts. Traditionally the tea is consumed directly from the gaiwan by using the lid to retain the leaves. For more precise tasting, we alter the technique slightly by filtering the liquor into another cup when each infusion is ready. This gives us more control over the process.

PREPARING TEA IN A GAIWAN

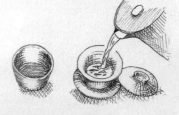

1. Preheat the gaiwan for several seconds with hot water and empty it. Measure 1 to 2 tsp. (3 to 5g) of tea into the gaiwan.

2. Heat the water to the required temperature and pour over the leaves.

Infusion in a Gaiwan	Amount per Gaiwan	Temperature	Duration of Infusion	Notes
Small-leaf Chinese green tea	1 to 2 tsp. (2.5 to 5 g)	75 to 85° C	1st : 10 sec 2nd : 10 sec 3rd : 20 sec	The infusion time will vary according to the quantity of leaves used and the volume of the gaiwan.
Large-leaf Chinese green tea	1 to 3 tsp. (3 to 6 g)	75 to 85° C	1st : 20 sec 2nd : 20 sec 3rd : 40 sec	

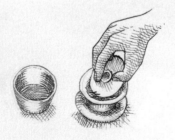

3. Infuse for 10 to 45 seconds.

4. Transfer the liquid into a cup. Taste. Repeat the infusions by varying the time to achieve the desired intensity.

JAPANESE TECHNIQUE

With the appearance of loose-leaf tea in the seventeenth century, a new way of drinking tea was introduced in Japan. Until then, the tea consumed on the archipelago was in powder form, known today as Matcha. It was prepared according to a strict code that very influential tea masters had established for the ceremony. For many tea lovers who sought a less formal approach, loose-leaf tea infusion was a way to escape these constraints.

Though this infusion method was initially not bound by precise rules, it was nevertheless codified over the course of the nineteenth century, finally taking on a fixed form in the Senchado ("Way of Sencha") ceremony. The technique we are presenting here is a summary of this "way."

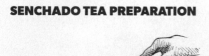

SENCHADO TEA PREPARATION

1. Preheat the teapot for several seconds with hot water. Empty out this water. Measure 3 to 5g of tea into the pot.

2. Prepare water between 65 and 75° C. To measure the exact quantity of water to be infused (around 100 ml), fill your cup first.

Senchado Infusion	Amount / 100 ml	Temperature	Examples of Infusion Durations	Notes
Japanese green tea	1 to 2 tsp. (3 to 5 g)	65 to 75° C	1st: 15 sec 2nd: 5 sec 3rd: 10 sec	The infusion time will vary depending upon the type and quality of the leaves used.

3. Pour the water from the cup onto the leaves in the pot and infuse for around 15 seconds.

4. Pour the infused liquor back into the cup. Be sure to empty the teapot completely to stop the infusion. Taste. Repeat the infusions to achieve the desired intensity.

2. WITHERING

Immediately after plucking, the leaves are taken to the factory for withering. This reduces the moisture content of the leaves. Several factors, such as room temperature and the use of fans, will influence the length of the process.

1. HARVESTING

For green teas, the harvest typically consists of the terminal bud and the two following leaves down the stem. In Japan, the harvest is mostly mechanized, while in China, it is generally still plucked manually.

3. FIXING

Fixing requires heating the leaves until the enzymes that cause oxidation have been neutralized. In Japan, steam is used for this stage, but in most other tea-producing countries, the leaves are heated in metal pans or cylinders with heat from a fire or with electrical elements.

5. DRYING

Drying removes the remaining moisture and captures the aromatic oils that were liberated during the rolling. After drying, only 2 to 7% of the initial moisture remains, stabilizing the leaves.

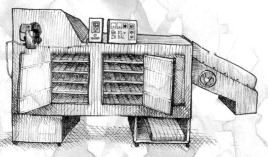

6. SORTING

The leaves are sifted either by hand or mechanically to remove dust and branches. This stage also separates leaves of different sizes into a range of grades.

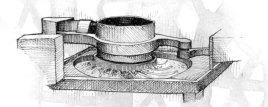

4. ROLLING

Rolling the leaves breaks the plant cells, releasing the aromatic oils. Depending on the type of machine used or the manual technique of the artisans, the leaves may be formed into flat, twisted, needle-shaped, or small pearl styles.

Although tea is consumed at every hour of the day in Asia, some green teas are more appropriate for particular occasions. Choosing a tea based on the hour of day, one's mood, the setting in which it will be consumed, and the persons with whom it will be shared is still the best way to fully appreciate each the unique virtues of each tea.

DAWN

Some passionate tea lovers get up at dawn to take advantage of the morning quiet and to enjoy their favourite tea on an empty stomach. The body is more sensitive at this hour and the infusion's multiple benefits will be more apparent. Dawn is a perfect moment for smooth and delicate grands crus. Drinking them first thing in the morning makes them all the more glorious.

Suggested Dawn Teas: Gyokuro, Kabusecha, Anji Bai Cha, Tai Ping Hou Kui

MORNING

If you were brought up in the English tradition in which black tea with sugar and milk is served, you may find it difficult to imagine green tea as your main breakfast beverage. But why not give it a try? Choose a brisk green tea with a full body. Green tea adds a great morning boost that pairs well with a large breakfast.

Suggested Morning Teas: Dong Shan, Kamairicha, Du Yun Mao Jian

AFTERNOON

Tea's gastronomic and stimulating qualities are particularly suitable for the afternoon hours. Some drink it for its digestive properties, others for its energizing effect, and all of those who have made it part of their everyday activities know that it greatly stimulates both the physical and intellectual capacities.

Suggested Afternoon Teas: Long Jing, Sencha Mobata, Wei Shan Mao Jian, Tan Huong

EVENING

If you are sensitive to caffeine, reduce your tea drinking in the evening; otherwise, you may risk trading several hours of sleep for hours of wakeful reflection. There are, however, some green teas with less caffeine content. Roasted green teas are a good choice for evening tea consumption.

Suggested Evening Teas: Hojicha Shizuoka, Huiming

TASTING INDEX

 Antioxidant (.moles /250 ml)   ● Caffeine (mg /250 ml)

ANJI BAI CHA
With its beautiful thread-like leaves, Anji Bai Cha is a treasure of refinement. Its sweet and slightly acidic flavours are accentuated by notes of pine nut and fruit, with a sublime floral finish.

 1800   N/A   p. 42

BAI HAO YIN ZHEN
Consisting solely of buds, this white tea produces a full and silky liquid. Its straw-and-ripe-banana notes are complemented by a refreshing flowery finish with chamomile accents.

 700   15   p. 56

BAI MU DAN
A white tea composed of downy buds and their first leaves, the woody character of its sweet liquid is balanced by a long finish of lily and cinnamon accents.

 1025   39   p. 56

BAI YE HUIMING
Created from a highly-prized modern cultivar, this tea is made up of fine buds and yellowish leaves. Full and silky, its liquid combines accents of buttered asparagus, fresh hazelnut, and delicate flowers.

 1530   N/A   p. 42

BI LUO CHUN
This famous tea from Jiangsu is comprised of fine, curly young shoots. Its velvety, thick, rich liquid reveals accents of spring flowers with nuances of clove, chocolate, and candied lemon.

 2105   53   p. 38

DONG SHAN
A pleasant everyday green tea, Dong Shan has a grassy, balanced, rich character. It is a full-bodied and clear liquid that is accentuated by hints of subtle cacao and slightly iodized notes.

 3180   62   p. 38

DU YUN MAO JIAN
With its contrasting silvery buds and curly dark green leaves, this tea from Guizhou Province is a pleasure to behold. Its slightly velvety, lively, and full-bodied liquid is complemented by pleasant accents of melon and fried spinach.

 N/A   N/A   p. 68

GYOKURO SHUIN
A very complex and aromatic tea with a dark green liquid, this type of Gyokuro has spinach flavours and marine notes evocative of wakame seaweed.

 1255   61   p. 106

HOJICHA SHIZUOKA

This tea is made with the large leaves picked at the end of the harvest period. The roasted leaves' brown colour is characteristic of Hoji-cha-type teas. Its honey taste is enhanced by notes of roasted nuts and bark.

HUANG SHAN MAO FENG

Grown in the majestic Yellow Mountains in Anhui Province, these tender young shoots with their open forms suggest a certain lightness. Huang Shan Mao Feng is a supple liquid characterized by a smooth texture and woody accents.

HUIMING

Well-balanced in both aromas and tannins, this tea from Zheijiang is accessible and refreshing. Its slightly oily liquor has a pleasant bitterness nuanced by the sweet fragrance of wild flowers.

HUO SHAN HUANG YA

This green tea's delicate leaves are certain to delight the palate. Its refreshing, zesty, and slightly acidic liquor is accompanied by heady floral fragrances.

JINGNING BAI CHA

The cultivar used to produce this high grade classic comes from wild tea plants reproduced by grafting. Its tender yellow-green leaves produce a smooth and delicately tan liquid with distinct roasted hazelnut accents.

JUN SHAN HUANG MAO JIAN

This Mao Jian-style yellow tea from Hunan Province consists of both buds and leaves. Its rosy, silky, and refined liquor is nuanced by a sensuous finish of marzipan.

JUN SHAN YIN ZHEN

Its magnificent buds come from Jun Shan Island in Hunan Province. It is produced using a traditional heaped-fermentation technique. Its delicate and slightly tart crystalline liquor is sustained by notes of pear and artichoke.

KABUSECHA TAKAMADO

This tea is a shade-grown cultivar from the Uji region of Japan. The velvety and sweet infusion features notes of green pea and cashew with a mildly marine aftertaste.

LONG JING SHI FENG

This high-quality tea from Zhejiang is famous for its delicate light green leaves. Its full-bodied and generous liquor is sustained by aromatic notes of roasted chestnuts and flowers.

LU AN GUA PIAN

These beautiful, long, and twisted leaves with bluish hues are handpicked one-by-one in Anhui Province. The leaves are dried with bamboo brushes, which are used to stir the leaves in heated vessels. The invigorating liquor is accompanied by notes of avocado and dandelion.

LUSHAN YUN WU

This green tea from Jiangxi Province is made up of attractive leaves and many buds. Its slightly sweet liquid reveals green pea and roasted chestnut aromas sustained by a soothing and delicate finish.

MATCHA CHOAN

Made from a high-grade Gyokuro, this Matcha is remarkably rich. Its aroma of fresh butter is light and subtle. Its white chocolate sweetness, milky flavour, and marine aromas make this an exquisitely balanced tea.

MATCHA UJI

The smooth liquor of the Matcha Uji has a sweet and brisk flavour with marine and grassy vegetal notes.

MENG DING HUANG YA

This Sichuan yellow tea consists almost entirely of buds. Its infusion reveals bold hazelnut aromas followed by a sweet vanilla finish.

NEPAL FIKKAL

The leaves and buds for this white tea from Nepal create a clear, slightly orange-tinged infusion that releases delicate woody and floral aromas. Its mouth-feel is brisk and smooth, providing a pleasant sensation of lightness.

SENCHA ASHIKUBO

Grown in the magnificent Ashikubo Valley, this typical asamushi tea is subjected to a long drying period. This results in a sweet and tasty liquor with aromas of exotic fruits and sweet corn.

SENCHA FUKAMUSHI AJI

This artisanally produced tea undergoes a prolonged desiccation, resulting in a liquor with a rich and smooth texture. The vivid green infusion has almond accents and a characteristic long finish.

SENCHA TSUKIGASE

Produced exclusively by an artisan grower from Nara Prefecture, this quality tea is made of irregular leaves. Its sweet and refreshing liquor has notes of wheatgrass and cashew culminating in a pronounced floral finish.

SENCHA YAMABUKI

The infusion of this Sencha's gold-coloured leaves produces a smooth and highly textured liquor with delicate marine accents and notes of snow peas.

TAI PING HOU KUI

This legendary tea consists of large textured and flattened leaves. Its smooth, brisk liquid is accentuated by subtle notes of orchids and roasted zucchini.

TAN HUONG

This tea is produced by a cooperative in Northern Vietnam. Rich in tannins, its invigorating liquid is accompanied by sweet and vegetal notes. Tan Huong is a variety that is certain to satisfy lovers of more robust teas.

TEMOMICHA

Prepared with care in a small volume of water, the infusion of its long needle-shaped leaves produces a rich and creamy liquid. Accentuated by a finish of heady floral fragrances, this tea has a finesse that only a handcrafted leaf can offer.

TUYET SAN

This green tea from Northern Vietnam is made up of long downy buds from very old, wild tea trees. Its light and sweet yellow liquid has a mineral texture accompanied by brisk artichoke accents and a refreshing fruity finish.

ZHU YE QING

Made up of superb, shiny, and uniform leaves, this prestigious Sichuan tea produces a vivid liquor with notes of bamboo sprouts accompanied by an acidic accent, floral fragrances, and a sweet finish.

---

*   Antioxidant (.moles/100 ml)

BIBLIOGRAPHY

Blofeld, John. *The Chinese Art of Tea*. Shambala, 1997.

Camellia Sinensis Tea House. *Tea: History, Terroirs, Varieties*. Firefly Books, 2011.

Chow, Kit and Ione Kramer. *All the Tea in China*. China Books, 1990.

Collective. *China: Homeland of Tea*. 1994.

Collective. *Tea for two. Les rituels du thé dans le monde*. Crédit Communal, 1999.

Heiss, Mary Lou and Robert J. *The Story of Tea: A Cultural History and Drinking Guide*. Ten Speed Press, 2007.

Iguichi, Kaisen. *Tea Ceremony*. Color Books, 1975.

Kakuzo, Okakura. *The Book of Tea*. Ed. Bruce Richardson. Benjamin Press, 2011.

Kuroda, Yukiaki and Yukihiko Hara. *Health Effects of Tea and Its Catechins*. Plenum Publishers, 2004.

Pasqualini, Dominique T. and Bruno Suet. *Le temps du thé*. Marval, 1999.

Soutel-Gouiffes, S. J. *La Voie des quatre Vertus (voie du thé). Expérience d'un itinéraire spirituel*. La Table d'Émeraude, 1994.

Wang, Ling. *Tea and Chinese Culture*. Long River Press, 2005.

ACKNOWLEDGEMENTS

We would like to extend our sincerest thanks to:

All of the tea growers and professionals in the tea industry who have welcomed us over the years, presented us with the fruits of their labour, and answered our endless questions with such great generosity.

Our many trusty, tea-savvy translators.

All of the scientists and researchers at Asia's research centers, who never hesitate to share their knowledge.

Our families and friends, who continue year after year to support us in our journey along this unusual path.

Jonathan Racine, for his literary skills, patience, attentive listening, and our unique authors/writer relationship.

Thanks to Bernard Schutze, for his impeccable initial translation of the book.

Sébastien Collin, for his inspiring corrections; Kazuyo Fukunishi, for the wagashi recipes; and Marie Bilodeau, for her invaluable artistic contribution.

The Montreal Botanical Garden and TransBioTech laboratories for their openness and enthusiastic participation in this project.

Finally, a big thanks to all of our passionate clients. You inspire us to do business differently. Your curiosity and encouragement fuels us to continue exploring the fascinating world of tea.

GREEN TEA AUTHORS
HUGO, JASMIN, FRANÇOIS AND KEVIN
INVITE YOU TO PERUSE THEIR VAST CATALOGUE
OF SEASONAL GRAND CRU TEAS AT
WWW.CAMELLIA-SINENSIS.COM